Mastering Skills for the TOEFL® iBT

Second Edition

Advanced **SPEAKING**

Mastering Skills for the TOEFL® iBT Second Edition
SPEAKING

Patrick Yancey · Casey Malarcher · Jeff Zeter

Acquisitions Editor: Tanya Shawlinski
Content Editor: J.K. Runner
Copy Editor: Moraig Macgillivray
Cover/Interior Design: Design Plus

Email: info@compasspub.com
http://www.compasspub.com

ISBN: 978-1-59966-358-6

13 12 11 10 9 8
15 14 13

Photo Credits
pp. 153, 156, 158, 160, 167, 170, 172 © Shutterstock Inc.
p. 174 © iStock International Inc.

Second Edition

Mastering Skills for the TOEFL® iBT

Advanced

Patrick Yancey · Casey Malarcher · Jeff Zeter

Table of Contents

Introduction to the TOEFL® iBT

What to Expect on the TOEFL®

The TOEFL® (Test of English as a Foreign Language) is an Internet-based test designed to assess English proficiency in non-native speakers who want to achieve academic success and communicate effectively in English. Most people take the TOEFL® iBT to gain admission into universities and colleges where instruction is in English. Additionally, many employers and government agencies use the scores to determine a person's English ability. It is not meant to test academic knowledge or computer ability, and as such, questions are always based on information found in the test (computer tutorials are available for those not familiar with personal computers). We have designed this practice book to be as similar as possible to the actual TOEFL® iBT in format and appearance in order to better prepare you for the test.

The TOEFL® iBT is divided into four sections: reading, listening, speaking, and writing.

Major Changes to the Internet-Based TOEFL® (iBT)

- **General**
  - ⇨ The test measures all four language skills equally; a speaking section is included.
  - ⇨ The Test of Spoken English® (TSE®) will now be part of the TOEFL®. Test takers will no longer take the TSE® as a separate test.
  - ⇨ Order of sections on the test:

    Reading
    Listening
    (10-minute break)
    Speaking
    Writing
  - ⇨ The test is approximately four hours long and is taken in one day.
  - ⇨ Tests are administered through the Internet in Educational Testing Service (ETS) test centers around the world.
  - ⇨ There is no structure section, as there was in previous tests.
  - ⇨ Note-taking is allowed in every section, and is not marked.
  - ⇨ The test is a linear exam, not computer adaptive; each test taker receives the same range of questions.
  - ⇨ The scores will be viewed online.

- **Reading / Listening**
  - ⇨ Passages for the reading and listening sections are longer than those in the computer-based test (CBT). Refer to the introduction of individual sections for further details.

- **Speaking / Writing**
  - ⇨ Tasks for the speaking and writing sections include integrated questions that require more than one skill to complete, i.e., reading and/or listening, then speaking or writing.
  - ⇨ For the speaking section, test takers speak into a microphone, and their responses are digitized and sent to the ETS Online Scoring Network.
  - ⇨ For the writing section, test takers must type their responses.

The TOEFL® iBT Format

Section	Number of Questions	Time (minutes)	Score
Reading	3–5 passages • 12–14 questions each • 700 words per passage	60–100	30 points
Listening	4–6 lectures • 6 questions each • 500–800 words (4–6 min.) 2–3 conversations • 5 questions each • 400–500 words (2–3 min.)	60–90	30 points
BREAK		10	
Speaking	2 independent tasks • 1 personal experience • 1 preference/choice 2 integrated tasks (Read-Listen-Speak) • Reading 100 words • Conversation 200 words (1–2 min.) • Lecture 200–300 words (1–2 min.) 2 integrated tasks (Listen-Speak) • Conversation 200 words (1–2 min.) • Lecture 200–300 words (1–2 min.)	20	30 points
Writing	1 independent task 1 integrated task (Read-Listen-Write) - Reading 250–300 words - Lecture 250–300 words (2 min.)	50	30 points

Study Tips

The only way to be certain of an excellent TOEFL® score is to be able to read, write, understand, and speak English like an educated native speaker. You have no doubt been developing your ability in these areas for many years now. Unfortunately, this is not something one can accomplish by studying in the traditional way. However, research conducted over the years by applied linguists, psychologists, and educators has yielded a considerable amount of information on the best methods for refining these skills for the purposes of standardized tests. By keeping the following study tips in mind, you can optimize your study habits and achieve the highest possible scores with the level of language proficiency you have obtained.

- Prepare a study area for yourself. This should include the following:
  - ⇨ A comfortable chair and spacious table or desk
  - ⇨ Suitable lighting
  - ⇨ Good ventilation and air quality—an open window or a house plant are good ideas
  - ⇨ An area free of distractions such as outside noise, television, or radio (unless you are using the television or radio to study)
  - ⇨ Proper space to keep all the materials you will need when studying, such as books, paper, pens, pencils, a tape recorder or other recording device, and if possible, a computer with Internet access

- Study regularly over a long period of time. Do not study to the point of exhaustion, as this has been shown to be ineffective in retaining information.

- "Cramming," i.e., studying intensely for a short period of time before an exam, is not effective, as it strains your general health and well-being and does not lead to long-term retention of information or skills.

- Psychologists have discovered a principle called "state-specific memory." This means you remember things better in the same conditions in which you learned them. For example, if you always study math at night, you will do better on a math exam taken at night. Use this concept to your advantage. If you know when and under what conditions you will take the TOEFL®, simulate these in your study environment and habits. For instance, if you plan to take the TOEFL® on a Saturday afternoon, then make it a point to study in the afternoons.

- Be well rested on the day of the exam. Do not stay up all night studying. Also, eat healthy foods including fruits and vegetables.

- Be relaxed and confident. Do the best that you can and do not worry excessively about any mistakes or uncertainties.

- Be well rested on the day of the exam. Do not stay up all night studying. Also, eat healthy foods including fruits and vegetables.

- Be relaxed and confident. Do the best that you can and do not worry excessively about any mistakes or uncertainties.

Registering For the TOEFL®

Students must get registration information for the TOEFL®. Registration information can be obtained online at the ETS website. The Internet address is www.ets.org/toefl. The website provides information such as testing locations, costs, and identification requirements. The website also provides other test-preparation material.

The registration information, such as the test center location, identification requirements, and costs, will vary depending on the country in which you take the test. Be sure to follow these requirements carefully. If you do not have the proper requirements in order, you may not be able to take the test. Remember that if you register online, you will need to have your credit card information ready.

What TOEFL® Scores Are Used For

The primary use of TOEFL® scores is for acceptance into universities, colleges, and other institutions where English is the main language of instruction. It is estimated that about 4,400 such institutions require TOEFL® scores for admission.

The highest possible score on the iBT is 120 points. Different institutions will have their own specific score requirements for admission. For that reason, it is very important to check with each institution individually to find out what its admission requirements are. For example, a passing score at one university may not be a passing score at another university. It is the responsibility of the student to find out what the requirements are for each institution.

Although TOEFL® scores are used primarily to satisfy the admissions requirements of universities, they are also necessary when applying for certain kinds of jobs. Many government agencies as well as multinational corporations require applicants to submit TOEFL® scores. Even English-teaching institutes may request TOEFL® scores in order to place students at the appropriate level of instruction.

Certainly, doing well on the TOEFL® can be very helpful for students in both their academic and professional careers. However, success requires consistent and dedicated practice. We hope that you will take full advantage of this practice book and study hard. Your hard work and dedication will provide you with the best opportunity to do well on the TOEFL® and meet your goals for the future.

Academic Subjects in the TOEFL®

The following is a list of academic subject areas typically seen in the TOEFL®:

Humanities	Social Sciences	Biological Sciences	Physical Sciences
Archaeology	Anthropology	Agriculture	Astronomy
Architecture	Business	Anatomy	Chemistry
Art History	Economics	Biology	Computer Science
Fine Arts	Education	Botany	Engineering
Linguistics	Geography	Entomology	Geology
Literature	History	Environmental Science	Mathematics
Music	Political Science	Medicine	Oceanography
Philosophy	Psychology	Zoology	Physics
	Public Health		
	Sociology		
	Urban Studies		

The TOEFL® iBT Speaking Section

The prompts for speaking questions on the TOEFL® iBT can be categorized into six types:

Question	Time			
	Reading	Listening	Preparation	Speaking
Independent Q1			15 seconds	45 seconds
Independent Q2				
Integrated Q3	45 seconds	1–2 minutes	30 seconds	60 seconds
Integrated Q4				
Integrated Q5		1–2 minutes	30 seconds	60 seconds
Integrated Q6				

The purpose of the speaking section is to evaluate your ability to speak coherently both on your opinions and experiences as well as on information that you have read or heard. The speaking questions fall into two categories: independent and integrated. For the two independent speaking questions, you should draw upon your own experience and knowledge. For the remaining four speaking questions, you will speak about what you read and/or hear. Your ideas need to be well organized, and the vocabulary and grammar you use must be accurate enough to be easily understood.

In particular, each question type will require test takers to organize their ideas and speak toward different goals:

Question	Task	Materials	Length	Tasks
1	Independent	none		Describe your experience.
2	Independent	none		Give your opinion and explain why you think this.
3	Integrated	Reading Conversation	100 words 200 words 60–90 seconds	Restate the opinion of the speaker and the examples used.
4	Integrated	Reading Lecture	100 words 200 words 60–90 seconds	Explain how the example from the lecture supports or refutes the passage.
5	Conversation-based	Conversation	300 words 90–120 seconds	Restate suggestions and tell which you think is better.
6	Lecture-based	Lecture	300 words 90–120 seconds	Summarize what you heard.

Study Tips for Speaking

- Master the North American English phonetic system as best as you can. Pay special attention to difficult distinctions such as: b/v, f/p, r/l, s/th, j/z, si/shi, the vowel sounds in bat/bet, it/eat, and shirt/short. Also, practice pronouncing the diphthongs (combined vowels) as one short, continuous sound rather than two separate ones. These include the sounds in the following: ail, bye, boy, and house.
- Practice speaking with a North American inflection. This involves moving the lips and opening the mouth wider, and speaking more from the mouth and nose than from the back of the throat.
- Practice using the pauses and intonations you learn when studying for the listening section of the TOEFL® iBT.
- Practice speaking at home. Use one of the independent writing topics as a speaking topic. Give yourself 15 seconds of preparation time. Use this time to think of your main idea and details or examples to support it. Speak for approximately 45 seconds on the topic. Also practice with 30 seconds of preparation time and one minute of speaking time, as this will be the case for the integrated exercises.

Test Management

- You will speak into a microphone attached to a headset.
- Independent Speaking questions come first.
- You can take notes and then use them when preparing your response.
- Check the time with the clock shown in the title bar on the computer screen.

How Speaking Will Be Scored

ETS graders will score test takers' responses according to the following scale:

Score	General Description	Key Points
4	The response answers the question or prompt well. The speaker is easy to understand and there are only minor mistakes with grammar or pronunciation.	Fluent speech that is easy to understand and follow, appropriate use of grammar and vocabulary, ideas are explained clearly
3	The response answers the question or prompt, but not all of the ideas are fully developed. The speaker can be understood, but there are some clearly noticeable mistakes in speaking.	At least two of these problems are present: poor pronunciation, poor pace of speech, wrong word choice, limited use of grammar structures, or incorrect grammar
2	The response gives only a basic or minimal answer to the question or prompt. Most sentences can be understood, but some effort is required by the listener because speech is not fluent and pronunciation is not accurate. Some ideas are not clearly explained.	At least two of these problems are present: poor pronunciation, choppy speech (not fluent), incorrect word choices, basic grammar, poor use of grammar, only basic ideas are presented, explanation is absent or limited
1	The response is very short, does not show full understanding of the question or prompt, and is hard for the listener to understand.	At least two of these problems are present: poor pronunciation, choppy speech (not fluent), long or frequent pauses, poor grammar, use of obviously practiced or formulaic expressions, lots of repetition of expressions in the question or prompt
0	There is no response or the response is not related to the question or prompt.	No response to grade, or response is not related to the question or prompt

Preview

Question 1

The following is a sample Question 1 similar to the one you will see when you take the test. You will first see a prompt on your screen describing the task.

Describe an important accomplishment from your past. Why was this accomplishment important to you? Include specific reasons and examples to support your answer.

You will then have have 30 seconds to prepare a response and 60 seconds to speak your response into the microphone. A sample outline of a response can be found below.

Sample Outline

Introduction:

Thesis statement

Body:

Reason 1

Topic sentence

Reasons, examples, and details

Reason 2

Topic sentence

Reasons, examples, and details

Sample Response

Thesis statement

One of my significant childhood accomplishments was learning how to ride a bicycle successfully.

Topic sentence

This was important because I first learned how hard work can pay off. I spent many days learning how to ride a bicycle. Then one day I was able to ride it without falling. I realized that when I practiced hard enough at something, I could achieve it.

Reasons, examples, and details

Topic sentence

Secondly, it helped me to obtain a level of independence. Now that I could ride a bicycle, I could go to different places by myself without having to depend on my parents for a ride. It made me a freer child.

Reasons, examples, and details

Question 2

The following is a sample Question 2 similar to the one you will see when you take the test. You will first see a prompt on your screen describing the task.

Many believe that it is important that children spend time participating in extracurricular activities. Others believe that it is more important that children spend most of their time studying. Which view do you believe? Include specific reasons and examples to support your answer.

You will then have 30 seconds to prepare a response and 60 seconds to speak your response into the microphone. A sample outline of a response can be found below.

Sample Outline

Introduction:

Thesis statement

Body:

Reason 1

Topic sentence

Reasons, examples, and details

Reason 2

Topic sentence

Reasons, examples, and details

Sample Response

Thesis statement

I believe it is important for children to spend some time participating in extracurricular activities.

Topic sentence

First of all, extracurricular activities let children develop their bodies as well as their minds. As a young child, most of the exercise I received was at after-school soccer games. Hence, I think children should participate in these types of activities so they can maintain their physical health.

Reasons, examples, and details

Topic sentence

Secondly, they help students figure out what they are good at and what they like to do. Playing in an after-school band allowed me to realize how much I loved music. Now I want to study music professionally in college. → Reasons, examples, and details

Question 3

The following is a sample Question 3 similar to the one you will see when you take the test. You will first see a short reading passage about a campus-related topic. You will have 45 seconds to read the announcement.

Announcement from the University Library

As of September 1, students who fail to return library books by the due date will not be allowed to register for classes until the books are returned and the late fees are paid in full. This past semester, we received a large number of overdue books, and we hope that the new policy will encourage more students to return books on time. In addition, the library would like to use all late fees collected under this policy to help fund an old books exhibit on the library's main floor.

After 45 seconds, you will be asked to listen to a conversation about the passage you just read. Read the conversation below. Keep in mind that this conversation will only be heard on the real test and will not appear on your screen.

M: Did you see this notice from the library? I'm going to have to be more careful about returning books on time.

W: Well, I think it's a good thing. It seems like every time I want to check out a book, it's not available. It's almost always because someone didn't return it by the due date. Then I have to request the book back, and it takes several days to get it.

M: Sounds like a major pain.

W: So this new policy will get more students to return their books by the due date.

M: I bet it will. No one wants to miss class registration or accumulate fines just because of an overdue library book.

W: Right. Plus, my history professor said that the library is going to try to fund an exhibit of books over a hundred years old. I bet it could raise enough money to fund future exhibits as well.

M: That'd be pretty nice.

W: Yeah, the library staff always comes up with neat exhibits. And I've found that a lot of them can even be helpful for class projects. They've helped me in the past.

After the conversation concludes, you will see a prompt on your screen similar to the one below.

The woman expresses her opinion of the announcement made by the library. State her opinion and explain the reasons she gives for holding that opinion.

You will have 30 seconds to prepare a response and 60 seconds to speak your response into the microphone. A sample outline of a response can be found on the next page.

Sample Outline

Introduction:

Summary and speaker's opinion

Body:

Reason 1

Topic sentence

Reasons, examples, and details

Reason 2

Topic sentence

Reasons, examples, and details

Sample Response

The woman thinks that the new library policy not to allow students to register until they return library books and pay overdue fees is a good idea.

Summary and speaker's opinion

Topic sentence

She complains that she often cannot check out the books she wants because students do not return them on time. Then she has to request the book back, which takes time. She thinks that the new policy will encourage students to return the books by the due date.

Reasons, examples, and details

Topic sentence

She also thinks that collecting fees will help the library fund other exhibits in addition to the one they are planning. She mentions that these exhibits have helped her with past projects.

Reasons, examples, and details

Question 4

The following is a sample Question 4 similar to the one you will see when you take the test. You will first see a short reading passage about an academic topic. You will have 45 seconds to read the passage.

Extroversion Versus Introversion

According to modern personality theory, there are two fundamental types of people: introverts and extroverts. Extroverts are people who are predominantly concerned with the world outside of themselves. They tend to enjoy social interactions and are naturally enthusiastic, talkative, and assertive. Introverts, on the other hand, are largely interested in what goes on in their own minds. They tend to be quiet, reserved, less outgoing, and do not socialize as much.

Recent evidence has shown that these personality differences are the result of physiological differences in the body. Differences exist between the brains of introverts and extroverts. Also, introverts and extroverts use energy differently.

After 45 seconds, you will be asked to listen to a lecture about the passage you just read. Read the lecture below. Keep in mind that this lecture will only be heard on the real test and will not appear on your screen.

M: Personality differences, like introversion and extroversion, are actually consequences of physiological differences.

Recent studies show that, in general, extroverts and introverts have more activity in different areas of the brain. Researchers studied which areas of the brain were activated by looking at how much blood flows to different brain regions. The more that blood flows to a certain area, the more that area is activated. The studies found that introverts have more blood flow to areas that are responsible for internal processing, like remembering and problem solving. Conversely, extroverts have more activity in areas used for sensory processing, like listening or watching. So it's not surprising that introverts are inwardly focused while extroverts seek social activities.

Introverts and extroverts also differ in how their bodies use energy. Extroverts use up energy really quickly and they recharge their energy by engaging in social activities . . . which is why an extrovert can jump from one conversation to another or from party to party and still want to go dancing at two in the morning. Introverts, however, are energy conservers. Lots of social activities make them tired, and they have to spend some time being quiet by themselves to regain their energy. This is why many introverts will decide to leave a dinner party early so that they can go home and read a book or write a letter before going out again.

After the lecture concludes, you will see a prompt on your screen similar to the one below.

The professor describes two differences between introverts and extroverts. Explain how these differences influence personality.

You will then have 30 seconds to prepare a response and 60 seconds to speak your response into the microphone. A sample outline of a response can be found below.

Sample Outline

Introduction:

Summary of the lecture's main point

Body:

Reason 1

Topic sentence

Details from the lecture

Reason 2

Topic sentence

Details from the lecture

Sample Response

Summary of lecture's main point

The reading and the professor both state that extroversion and introversion are caused by physiological differences.

Topic sentence

The professor says that one difference between introverts and extroverts is the area of the brain that is most activated. In introverts, there is more activity in brain areas used for internal processing, which makes them more inwardly focused. In extroverts, there is more activity in areas used for sensory processing, which makes them more social.

Details from lecture

Topic sentence

Another difference between introverts and extroverts is how their brains use energy. Extroverts use up energy quickly and regain energy through socializing. Introverts conserve energy and regain energy by being alone. So extroverts tend to seek out social activities while introverts are more likely to spend more time by themselves.

Details from lecture

Question 5

The following is a sample Question 5 similar to the one you will see when you take the test. You will listen to a conversation between two students about a campus-related problem. Read the conversation below. Keep in mind that this conversation will only be heard on the real test and will not appear on your screen.

W: Hey, Carl. How do you like your new roommate?
M: He's OK. He's a really neat person and everything. There's just one problem.
W: What's that?
M: Well, he's a mathematics major. He just loves graphs and numbers. Anyway, he's been hanging these really ugly graphs and charts on all the dorm room's walls.
W: And that bothers you because you're an art major, right?
M: Exactly. Besides, I get enough of that stuff in my own math classes. I don't want to have to look at it while I'm relaxing, too.
W: Can't you just ask him to take them down?
M: Yeah, I was thinking of that. The thing is, I don't want to hurt his feelings. Plus, he's a really good roommate.
W: What about establishing some boundaries?
M: What do you mean?
W: There are four walls in your room. Tell your roommate that he can put his ugly posters on two walls. Then you can put your stuff on the other two walls.
M: I'll have to think about that. I'd have to tell him to stop taking up all the walls with his stuff. Even worse, I'd still have to look at two ugly walls. Those graphs and charts really bother me.
W: Hmm. Well, I guess you'll have to decide which option will work better for you.

After the conversation concludes, you will see a prompt on your screen similar to the one below.

The students discuss two possible solutions to the man's problem. Describe the problem. Then state which of the two solutions you prefer and explain why.

You will have 30 seconds to prepare a response and 60 seconds to speak your response into the microphone. A sample outline of a response can be found on the next page.

Sample Outline

Introduction:

Summary of the problem
Suggestions
Your preferred solution

Body:

Reason 1

Topic sentence
Reasons, examples, and details

Reason 2

Topic sentence
Reasons, examples, and details

Sample Response

Summary of problem

Suggestions

The man's roommate is putting up ugly graphs and charts on the walls. The woman suggests that he either ask his roommate to remove them completely or ask his roommate to limit his charts to two walls. I think the first option is the better one.

Your preferred solution

Topic sentence

First, I do not think the man should have to look at graphs and charts that he finds ugly up on his walls. It is his room, too, so he has a right to look at things that he finds pleasing.

Reasons, examples, and details

Topic sentence

Secondly, I think it is better for the man to be honest with his roommate. If they want to have a good relationship, they need to be able to talk to each other openly about things that bother them.

Reasons, examples, and details

Question 6

The following is a sample Question 6 similar to the one you will see when you take the test. You will listen to a lecture about an academic topic. Read the lecture below. Keep in mind that this lecture will only be heard on the real test and will not appear on your screen.

M: Scientists have long believed that one of the key differences between humans and all other animals is episodic memory—the kind of memory that lets us remember past events, times, places—even past emotions. Basically, they thought that we have it and that animals do not. But recent experiments have led many scientists to conclude that some animals actually do have episodic memory.

Several of these experiments have been carried out on a type of bird called a scrub jay. The experiments were designed to test whether scrub jays can recall past events and use what they remember to plan for the future. In one experiment, for example, researchers left out two types of food—worms and peanuts—for the jays to store for later use. When the birds dug up the worms, they found that many of them had spoiled. From then on, they dug up peanuts instead since they found that the peanuts were still good. This change in behavior led the researchers to believe that the birds remembered finding the spoiled worms in the past. Thus, they avoided digging them up in the future.

Other experiments have studied episodic memory in non-human primates, such as chimps and gorillas. There was one experiment, for example, that was conducted on a domesticated chimpanzee named Panzee at Georgia State University in Atlanta. During the experiment, researchers hid about thirty different items—items like fruits, balloons, and rubber snakes. They hid them one at a time—all while Panzee was watching from inside her cage. In more than ninety percent of the cases, Panzee correctly identified where each item was hidden. She directed her caretakers to each place the toys and fruits were hidden. This showed that she could recall the memory of the researchers hiding the items.

After the lecture concludes, you will see a prompt on your screen similar to the one below.

Using points and examples from the lecture, describe two cases in which animals exhibit episodic memory.

You will have 30 seconds to prepare a response and 60 seconds to speak your response into the microphone. A sample outline of a response can be found on the next page.

Sample Outline

Introduction:

Main topic

Body:

Key point 1

Topic sentence

Reasons, examples, and details

Key point 2

Topic sentence

Reasons, examples, and details

Sample Response

The professor says that recent experiments have led scientists to believe that animals, and not just humans, have episodic memory, or memories of past places and events.

Main topic

Topic sentence

One set of experiments showed that scrub jays have episodic memory. Researchers found that the jays can remember past events, such as finding spoiled worms, and use those memories to change their behavior. For example, after the jays initially dug up the worms and found them spoiled, they dug up stored peanuts instead of worms from then on.

Reasons, examples and, details

Topic sentence

Other experiments have studied episodic memory in non-human primates. One experiment studied a chimpanzee named Panzee, who remembered which toys and foods the researchers had hidden and where they had hidden them. Both these experiments show that certain animals have episodic memory.

Reasons, examples, and details

Part 1

Thinking and Speaking

- **Chapter 1** Independent Speaking: Organizing Speech
- **Chapter 2** Integrated Speaking: Synthesizing Information
- **Chapter 3** Integrated Speaking: Stating Opinions and Summarizing
- **Vocabulary Review 1**
- **Vocabulary Review 2**

Chapter 1 Independent Speaking: Organizing Speech

Necessary Skills

- Describing a personal experience or expressing a personal preference
- Organizing ideas
- Expressing a clear topic statement and supporting points
- Speaking clearly and accurately with knowledge of grammar, vocabulary, and pronunciation

Strategies

Though preparation time is limited in the speaking portion of the test, it is nevertheless important to use this time to plan the organization of your response. This way, your response will be more relevant and coherent. An organizational process for preparing your speech is detailed below. In each step, there are certain things to keep in mind.

Process	Strategy
Read the prompt and understand the task.	Be sure that you understand the question and what it requires you to do.
Identify the main idea and create a topic statement.	Decide on the main idea or choose a position. Use the relevant parts of the prompt in making your topic statement.
Brainstorm and select supporting ideas.	Quickly think of supporting ideas from your own experiences. Choose ideas that most clearly support your topic statement.
Organize the ideas.	Arrange your ideas, putting them in order from most important to least important.

Chapter 1

Q1 Practice 1 – Personal Experience

▶ Step 1

Read the prompt below. Write down your answer and related key points in the blanks.

> Describe a city you visited in your past that you found fascinating. Why did you enjoy your visit so much? Include specific reasons and examples to support your answer.

A fascinating city that I visited in my past was ______________________________

Reason 1: I enjoyed visiting there because ______________________________

____

____

Reason 2: Another reason I enjoyed visiting there is ______________________________

____

____

Read the related ideas and expressions below. Add at least two of your own.

Related Ideas and Expressions

city:

town, metropolis, settlement, ______________, ______________

visit:

stay, vacation, experience, ______________, ______________

fascinating:

captivating, charming, incredible, ______________, ______________

enjoy:

esteem, fancy, appreciate, ______________, ______________

originate:
to begin to exist for the first time

ancestor:
someone related to you who lived a long time ago

firsthand:
obtained directly by doing something oneself

date back:
to have begun at a certain time in the past

captivate:
to interest someone very much

Step 2

Listen to a sample response. Write down any useful expressions. Track 1

Notes

Step 3

Now create your own response using words and expressions from Steps 1 and 2. Use the prompts below to help you.

A fascinating city that I visited in my past was ____________________. I enjoyed myself there because ______________________________________. I had always wanted ______________ ____________________. By traveling there, ______________________________________ ____________________. I also enjoyed ____ _____________. Many ____. These ______________ captivated me, and I _______________________________________.

Step 4

Read the response you wrote above out loud. Try to read slowly and clearly. Practice saying the whole response several times. Then close your book and say the response without looking at the words.

Practice 2 – Personal Experience

▸ Step 1

Read the prompt below. Write down your answer and related key points in the blanks.

> What type of work would you like to choose as a career? Why would you make this choice? Include specific reasons and examples to support your answer.

The job that I would like to choose as a career is ______________________________

Reason 1: ______________________________

____

Reason 2: ______________________________

____

Read the related ideas and expressions below. Add at least two of your own.

Related Ideas and Expressions

type:

kind, sort, category, ____________, ____________

job:

career, occupation, profession, ____________, ____________

choose:

decide, pick, prefer, ____________, ____________

enable:

allow, cause, make possible, ____________, ____________

photographer:
someone who takes photographs

enable:
to give someone the opportunity to do something

remote:
far away from cities or towns

diverse:
different from each other

habitat:
the place where a certain animal normally lives

Step 2

Listen to a sample response. Write down any useful expressions. **Track 2**

Notes

____
____
____
____
____
____
____
____

Step 3

Now create your own response using words and expressions from Steps 1 and 2. Use the prompts below to help you.

For my career, I would choose to be ______________________. I would prefer this job because ____. ______________________ would allow me to ____. Such a career ____. I would get to ____.

The experiences ____.

Step 4

Read the response you wrote above out loud. Try to read slowly and clearly. Practice saying the whole response several times. Then close your book and say the response without looking at the words.

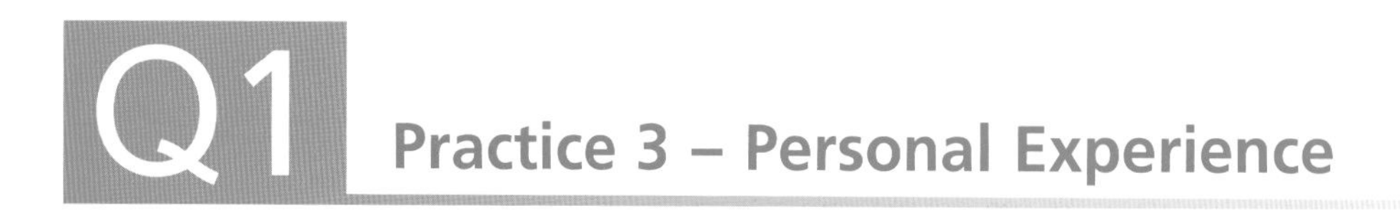

Q1 Practice 3 – Personal Experience

Step 1

Read the prompt below. Write down your answer and related key points in the blanks.

> Often a bad situation teaches us an important life lesson. Describe an important lesson that you learned from a bad situation. Include specific reasons and examples to support your answer.

One bad situation in my past that taught me an important life lesson was ______________________

____.

I feel that this situation helped me learn an important life lesson because ______________________

____

Reason 1: ____

____

Example: ____

Reason 2: ____

____

Example: ____

Read the related ideas and expressions below. Add at least two of your own.

Related Ideas and Expressions

bad:
awful, negative, dreadful, ______________, ______________

situation:
occurrence, state, condition, ______________, ______________

important:
vital, crucial, key, ______________, ______________

lesson:
message, skill, warning, ______________, ______________

obtain:
to get something

goal:
something that one hopes to achieve

summit:
the top of a mountain

blizzard:
a storm with lots of snow and high winds

exhausted:
very tired

Step 2

Listen to a sample response. Write down any useful expressions. Track 3

Notes

Step 3

Now create your own response using words and expressions from Steps 1 and 2. Use the prompts below to help you.

A bad situation recently taught me that ____. I learned this while ______________________. We wanted ______________________________________. ______________. However, ______________________. When ______________________________, ______________________. I learned that ______________________________.

Step 4

Read the response you wrote above out loud. Try to read slowly and clearly. Practice saying the whole response several times. Then close your book and say the response without looking at the words.

Chapter 1

Q2 Practice 1 – Personal Preference

▸ Step 1

Read the prompt below. Write down your answer and related key points in the blanks.

> Would you prefer to live in the mountains or near the ocean? Include specific reasons and examples to support your answer.

I would rather ______________________________

Reason 1: ______________________________

Example: ______________________________

Reason 2: ______________________________

Example: ______________________________

Read the related ideas and expressions below. Add at least two of your own.

Related Ideas and Expressions

prefer:

like better, rather, desire, ______________, ______________

live:

dwell, occupy, abide, ______________, ______________

mountain:

alpine, peak, cliff, ______________, ______________

water sports:

sailing, diving, water skiing, ______________, ______________

skiing:
a winter sport where a person slides over the snow on thin objects called skis

drift:
to be pushed along slowly by the water's movement

endure:
to suffer something that is difficult or unpleasant

maritime:
near the ocean

alpine:
relating to mountains

Step 2

Listen to two sample responses. Write down any useful expressions. Track 4

Notes

Step 3

Now create your own response using words and expressions from Steps 1 and 2. Use the prompts below to help you.

I would prefer to live somewhere that is near ______________________. Then ________ ______________________. ______________________ ______________. It is very ______________________. In addition, ______ ______________________. ______________________, and ______________________.

Step 4

Read the response you wrote above out loud. Try to read slowly and clearly. Practice saying the whole response several times. Then close your book and say the response without looking at the words.

Practice 2 – Personal Preference

▸ Step 1

Read the prompt below. Write down your answer and related key points in the blanks.

Some people enjoy having many friends. Others prefer to have a few close friends. Which would you prefer? Include specific reasons and examples to support your answer.

I prefer to have ____________________

Reason 1: ____________________

Example: ____________________

Reason 2: ____________________

Example: ____________________

Read the related ideas and expressions below. Add at least two of your own.

Related Ideas and Expressions

friends:

playmates, comrades, acquaintances, ____________, ____________

relationship:

association, friendship, link, ____________, ____________

difficult:

complicated, tricky, challenging, ____________, ____________

support:

encourage, maintain, help, ____________, ____________

overwhelming:
emotionally overpowering

divide:
to separate into different parts

consult:
to ask for information

isolated:
lonely or separate from other people

reach out:
to offer help to someone

Step 2

Listen to two sample responses. Write down any useful expressions. Track 5

Notes

Step 3

Now create your own response using words and expressions from Steps 1 and 2. Use the prompts below to help you.

I prefer to have ______________________________ rather than ______________________________. First of all, ______________________________, and ______________________________. In my experience, ______________________________. Secondly, I think ______________________________. When ______________________________.

Step 4

Read the response you wrote above out loud. Try to read slowly and clearly. Practice saying the whole response several times. Then close your book and say the response without looking at the words.

Practice 3 – Personal Preference

▸ Step 1

Read the prompt below. Write down your answer and related key points in the blanks.

> Some students like to work and earn money during the summer. Others like to have the summer off. Which would you prefer? Include specific reasons and examples to support your answer.

I prefer to spend my summer ______________________________

Reason 1: ______________________________

Example: ______________________________

Reason 2: ______________________________

Example: ______________________________

Read the related ideas and expressions below. Add at least two of your own.

Related Ideas and Expressions

money:

cash, funds, capital, ____________, ____________

summer vacation:

time off, holiday, leave, ____________, ____________

busy:

full of activity, tiring, diligent, ____________, ____________

boring:

uninteresting, nothing to do, tedious, ____________, ____________

remarkable:
unusual in a surprising way

afford:
having enough money to pay for something

recuperate:
to recover or restore

hang out:
to spend time with other people in a casual situation

novel:
a long written work of fiction

▸ Step 2

Listen to two sample responses. Write down any useful expressions. Track 6

Notes

____
____
____
____
____
____
____
____

▸ Step 3

Now create your own response using words and expressions from Steps 1 and 2. Use the prompts below to help you.

I would prefer to ____________________. This would ____________________. For example, last ____________________. It ____________________.

Also, if ____________________.

I would rather ____________________.

▸ Step 4

Read the response you wrote above out loud. Try to read slowly and clearly. Practice saying the whole response several times. Then close your book and say the response without looking at the words.

Chapter 2 Integrated Speaking: Synthesizing Information

Necessary Skills

- Understanding information in reading and listening passages
- Taking notes on important information and using this information in your spoken response
- Synthesizing background information with more specific information
- Synthesizing the information given in the reading and listening; using the points in the listening to highlight principles or differences in the reading
- Recognizing a speaker's purpose and attitude
- Paraphrasing information

Strategies

An organizational process for responding to a prompt based on integrated material is detailed below. In each step, there are certain things that you need to keep in mind.

Process	Strategy
Read and listen.	Take notes on important information in both the reading and listening passages.
Read the prompt and understand the task.	Identify relationships between information in the listening passage and the reading passage. What aspects of each does the prompt want you to discuss?
Organize the ideas.	Arrange the ideas from the listening and reading passages. Think of a topic sentence that reflects the information.

Practice 1 – Reading and Conversation

▶ Step 1

Read the following announcement. Write five keywords or key phrases that would be useful in explaining the information to someone else. While reading, try to guess what the conversation will be about.

Important Announcement

As of the end of this month, the university will no longer be providing free printing paper in the student computer lab. If students wish to print from the lab printer, they will be required to bring their own paper with them to the lab. We have found that students too often waste the paper the university provides by printing unscholarly materials including Internet chat conversations and airline tickets. Furthermore, the money the university will save on paper will be set aside for purchasing additional computers. This will allow the lab to accommodate more students.

printer:
a machine that prints computer documents

unscholarly:
unconnected with school or learning

chat:
talking with someone

purchase:
to buy

accommodate:
to provide room for someone

Keywords/ Key Phrases	
	_______________
	_______________
	_______________
	_______________
	_______________

Cover the passage and look at the keywords and key phrases only. Restate the passage in your own words.

Step 2

Now listen to a conversation related to the passage in Step 1. As you listen, take notes on important information. Write down five keywords or key phrases that would be useful in explaining this information to someone else. Track 7

Keywords/ Key Phrases	

distressing: upsetting

draft: something such as a research paper that requires changes before it is finished

journal: a document containing articles related to a specific profession or area of study

equipment: tools or machines needed to perform a specific activity

hassle: problem

Restate what you heard in the conversation using the notes or keywords you wrote above.

Step 3

Read the prompt below. Circle the most important ideas in your notes from both the reading and the conversation. Write down the main points you need to speak about.

The woman expresses her opinion about the university's decision. State her opinion and explain the reasons she gives for holding that opinion.

Opinion: The woman ______________________.

Reason 1: ______________________

Detail: ______________________

Reason 2: ______________________

Detail: ______________________

Step 4

Listen to a sample response. Write down any useful expressions. Track 8

Notes

Step 5

Now create your own response using words and expressions from Steps 3 and 4. Use the prompts below to help you.

The announcement says that students ______________________________ ______________. The woman ______________________________. First, she thinks that the university ______________________________. Everyone she knows ______________________________. Secondly, she thinks using the money saved on printer paper ______________________________. She feels that ______________________________ ______________________________. Therefore, they ______________________________.

Step 6

Read the response you wrote above out loud. Try to read slowly and clearly. Practice saying the whole response several times. Then close your book and say the response without looking at the words.

Q3 Practice 2 – Reading and Conversation

▸ Step 1

Read the following announcement. Write five keywords or key phrases that would be useful in explaining the information to someone else. While reading, try to guess what the conversation will be about.

Announcement from Campus Security

As of April 15, the price of parking tickets will be raised from $35 to $50 in part to deter students from parking illegally along the street. Parking along the street blocks traffic and prevents emergency vehicles, such as police cars and fire trucks, from easily accessing emergency fire lanes. We hope that a larger monetary penalty will help prevent students from blocking these lanes. We also hope that the larger fines will help raise money to build another student parking lot closer to the school so that students do not feel forced to park on the street.

deter: to discourage
emergency: an unexpected crisis or disaster
access: to get into a place
monetary: economic or financial
penalty: a punishment or a fine

Keywords/ Key Phrases	

Cover the passage and look at the keywords and key phrases only. Restate the passage in your own words.

Step 2

Now listen to a conversation related to the passage in Step 1. As you listen, take notes on important information. Write down five keywords or key phrases that would be useful in explaining this information to someone else. **Track 9**

Keywords/ Key Phrases	

substantial:
large or major

security:
the department or people in an organization that protect workers and buildings

current:
present or existing

waste:
to squander or use more of something than necessary

Restate what you heard in the conversation using the notes or keywords you wrote above.

Step 3

Read the prompt below. Circle the most important ideas in your notes from both the reading and the conversation. Write down the main points you need to speak about.

The man expresses his opinion about the university's decision. State his opinion and explain the reasons he gives for holding that opinion.

Opinion: ______________________

Reason 1: ______________________

Detail: ______________________

Reason 2: ______________________

Detail: ______________________

▸ Step 4

Listen to a sample response. Write down any useful expressions. Track 10

Notes

____
____
____
____
____
____
____
____

▸ Step 5

Now create your own response using words and expressions from Steps 3 and 4. Use the prompts below to help you.

The announcement says that ______________________________. The man ______________ because ______________________________. He thinks that by parking ______________________, students are ______________ because they are ______________________________. He also thinks that ______________________________. It takes him ______________ ______________________. If ______________________, students ______________________________.

▸ Step 6

Read the response you wrote above out loud. Try to read slowly and clearly. Practice saying the whole response several times. Then close your book and say the response without looking at the words.

Practice 3 – Reading and Conversation

▸ Step 1

Read the following announcement. Write five keywords or key phrases that would be useful in explaining the information to someone else. While reading, try to guess what the conversation will be about.

Announcement from the Registrar

The university has decided to switch from a paper-based course catalogue to an electronic course catalogue. Students will no longer have access to paper catalogues and will instead register for classes online using the online course catalogue posted on the university's website. This will save the university the high cost of paper and ink. Online registration will also be more convenient for students, who will be able to register for classes from their dorm computers. Students can register on their own time and will be saved a trip to the registrar's office.

registrar: the place at a university where official records are kept

catalogue: a list or directory

register: to sign up

post: to announce or advertise

dorm: a student's living quarters at a college or university

Keywords/ Key Phrases	

Cover the passage and look at the keywords and key phrases only. Restate the passage in your own words.

▸ Step 2

Now listen to a conversation related to the passage in Step 1. As you listen, take notes on important information. Write down five keywords or key phrases that would be useful in explaining this information to someone else. Track 11

Keywords/ Key Phrases	
	______
	______
	______
	______
	______
	______
	______

log on:
to access a website or network

network:
a set of computers that are connected to each other so each computer can send and receive information from other computers

inconvenient:
causing difficulties

flip:
turn over

navigate:
to find and follow a path or course

Restate what you heard in the conversation using the notes or keywords you wrote above.

▸ Step 3

Read the prompt below. Circle the most important ideas in your notes from both the reading and the conversation. Write down the main points you need to speak about.

> The man expresses his opinion about the university's decision. State his opinion and explain the reasons he gives for holding that opinion.

Opinion: ______

Reason 1: ______

Detail: ______

Reason 2: ______

Detail: ______

Step 4

Listen to a sample response. Write down any useful expressions. Track 12

Notes

Step 5

Now create your own response using words and expressions from Steps 3 and 4. Use the prompts below to help you.

The announcement says that the university will ____

______________. The man thinks that this is ____.

He feels ______________________________, like ____

____________. The man also thinks the online catalogues ______________________________________.

He mentions that ____. Many will _______________

____. He believes that _________________

_______________________________________. He concludes by saying ___________________________

____.

Step 6

Read the response you wrote above out loud. Try to read slowly and clearly. Practice saying the whole response several times. Then close your book and say the response without looking at the words.

Q4 Practice 1 – Reading and Lecture

Step 1

Read the following passage. Write five keywords or key phrases that would be useful in explaining the information to someone else. While reading, try to guess what the lecture will be about.

Color Perceptions

The symbolism of color may vary slightly from culture to culture, but psychologists have found that color affects emotions in a universal way. This means that different cultures tend to associate color with similar patterns of feelings and emotions. In fact, colors are divided into two groups depending on the kind of emotions they evoke. Colors on the red side of the color spectrum, known as warm colors, bring on feelings of warmth and comfort. Colors on the blue side of the color spectrum, known as cool colors, inspire feelings of calmness and confidence.

vary:
to differ

symbolism:
the use of symbols to represent something

universal:
occurring across the world

evoke:
suggest or call to mind

color spectrum:
the distribution of colors

Keywords/ Key Phrases	

Cover the passage and look at the keywords and key phrases only. Restate the passage in your own words.

Step 2

Now listen to a lecture related to the passage in Step 1. As you listen, take notes on important information. Write down five keywords or key phrases that would be useful in explaining this information to someone else. Track 13

Keywords/ Key Phrases	
	______
	______
	______
	______
	______
	______
	______

induce:
to bring on; to cause or create

opponent:
a person that is competing against you

authority:
power

menacing:
threatening or alarming

consultant:
one who gives professional advice

Restate what you heard in the lecture using the notes or keywords you wrote above.

Step 3

Read the prompt below. Circle the most important ideas in your notes from both the reading and the lecture. Write down the main points you need to speak about.

> The professor describes two types of color. Explain what these are and how they are used to affect mood.

Warm colors: ______

Example of how they are used: ______

Cool colors: ______

Example of how they are used: ______

Step 4

Listen to a sample response. Write down any useful expressions. Track 14

Notes

____
____
____
____
____
____
____
____

Step 5

Now create your own response using words and expressions from Steps 3 and 4. Use the prompts below to help you.

The reading mentions ____
____________________. It says that ____
__________. The professor then ____.
The professor mentions why ______________________________. They do this __________
____. The professor then mentions
____.

Step 6

Read the response you wrote above out loud. Try to read slowly and clearly. Practice saying the whole response several times. Then close your book and say the response without looking at the words.

Practice 2 – Reading and Lecture

Step 1

Read the following passage. Write five keywords or key phrases that would be useful in explaining the information to someone else. While reading, try to guess what the lecture will be about.

Dominance Hierarchies

In the animal kingdom, members of the same species that live in close proximity to one another often establish dominance hierarchies. A dominance hierarchy is a type of social structure in which certain individuals control the allocation of resources like food or mates. Everyone else in the group follows the leadership of these dominant individuals. In this way, dominance hierarchies serve to maintain order among its various members. They also allow individuals in a group to resolve conflicts. The survival of many social animal species depends on dominance hierarchies to properly function.

proximity: how near something is to another thing

social structure: a system of social organization based on certain patterns of social interaction

dominant: in control over others

allocation: how something is distributed or shared

conflict: a disagreement or an argument

Keywords/ Key Phrases	

Cover the passage and look at the keywords and key phrases only. Restate the passage in your own words.

Step 2

Now listen to a lecture related to the passage in Step 1. As you listen, take notes on important information. Write down five keywords or key phrases that would be useful in explaining this information to someone else. Track 15

Keywords/ Key Phrases	

baboon:
a large type of monkey living in Africa or Asia
rank:
a level or position
scarce:
rare
savanna:
a large flat area of land covered by grass
relaxed:
laid-back or casual

Restate what you heard in the lecture using the notes or keywords you wrote above.

Step 3

Read the prompt below. Circle the most important ideas in your notes from both the reading and the lecture. Write down the main points you need to speak about.

The professor discusses dominance hierarchies in baboons. Explain how this behavior is used in baboon societies.

Species that uses dominance hierarchies: ____________________

Point 1: ____________________

Example: ____________________

Point 2: ____________________

Example: ____________________

Step 4

Listen to a sample response. Write down any useful expressions. **Track 16**

Notes

____

____

____

____

____

____

____

____

Step 5

Now create your own response using words and expressions from Steps 3 and 4. Use the prompts below to help you.

The reading says that ____. The professor discusses ____ ______________________. There is ____ __________. The professor then says ____. This is important ______________________________. Therefore, ______________ ______________________________. Conversely, ______________________________.

Step 6

Read the response you wrote above out loud. Try to read slowly and clearly. Practice saying the whole response several times. Then close your book and say the response without looking at the words.

Practice 3 – Reading and Lecture

▸ Step 1

Read the following passage. Write five keywords or key phrases that would be useful in explaining the information to someone else. While reading, try to guess what the lecture will be about.

Plate Tectonics

According to the theory of plate tectonics, the Earth's crust is divided into huge plates that float atop the molten rock underneath. Geologists first recognized the existence of tectonic plates in 1915, when German geologist Alfred Wegener proposed the hypothesis of continental drift.

Wegener contended that all the continents were previously one large continent called Pangea. Over the course of history, Pangea broke apart, and the pieces drifted away to become the continents that exist today. Evidence that Pangea once existed can be found through fossils spread out across the different continents. Similar rock formations on different continents also lend credence to Wegener's hypothesis.

crust:
an outer layer of something

molten:
made liquid by heat

hypothesis:
an educated guess

continent:
one of the seven main landmasses on the Earth

contend:
to argue or assert

credence:
credibility; weight

Keywords/ Key Phrases	
	______________________
	______________________
	______________________
	______________________
	______________________

Cover the passage and look at the keywords and key phrases only. Restate the passage in your own words.

▸ Step 2

Now listen to a lecture related to the passage in Step 1. As you listen, take notes on important information. Write down five keywords or key phrases that would be useful in explaining this information to someone else. Track 17

Keywords/ Key Phrases	
	______
	______
	______
	______
	______
	______
	______

devise:
to plan or develop

jigsaw puzzle:
a game made up of differently shaped pieces that fit together to create a picture

fossil:
remains of an animal or plant in which the bones or tissue have been replaced by rock

deposit:
a concentration of mineral or rock

distinct:
clear or definite

Restate what you heard in the lecture using the notes or keywords you wrote above.

▸ Step 3

Read the prompt below. Circle the most important ideas in your notes from both the reading and the lecture. Write down the main points you need to speak about.

> The professor discusses the theory of continental drift. Explain what it is and how it is supported.

Continental drift: ______

Evidence 1: ______

Example: ______

Evidence 2: ______

Example: ______

Step 4

Listen to a sample response. Write down any useful expressions. Track 18

Notes

Step 5

Now create your own response using words and expressions from Steps 3 and 4. Use the prompts below to help you.

The passage first ______________________________ ______________________________. It states that ______________ ______________________________. The professor explains ______________ ______________________________. This led scientists ______________________________ ______________. The professor also states ______________________________ ________. This further ______________________________.

Step 6

Read the response you wrote above out loud. Try to read slowly and clearly. Practice saying the whole response several times. Then close your book and say the response without looking at the words.

Chapter 3 Integrated Speaking: Stating Opinions and Summarizing

Necessary Skills

- Understanding the key information in listening passages
- Taking notes on important information and using this information in your spoken response
- Paraphrasing information
- Expressing an opinion or preference
- Supporting an opinion with reasons or examples

Strategies

An organizational process for preparing your speech is detailed below. In each step, there are certain things to keep in mind.

Process	Strategy
Listen to a conversation or lecture.	Take notes on the key points and important details.
Read the prompt and understand the task.	Identify what you will need to discuss.
Organize the ideas.	Decide on your topic sentence and the supporting details. Be sure to include reasons and examples for any personal opinions expressed.

Q5 Practice 1 – Conversation

Step 1

Listen to a conversation. As you listen, take notes on the problem and the solutions suggested. Track 19

Problem: ____________________

____________________.

Solution 1: ____________________

____________________.

Solution 2: ____________________

____________________.

organic:
relating to living organisms

scholarship:
a grant of financial aid given to a student attending college

transcript:
a record of the student's classes and grades

GPA:
grade point average; the average grade earned by a student

ace:
to receive an A on a test or assignment

Step 2

Read the prompt below. Write down your opinion.

The students discuss two possible solutions to the woman's problem. Describe the problem. Then state which of the two solutions you prefer and explain why.

Problem: ____________________

Best solution: ____________________

Reason 1: ____________________

Reason 2: ____________________

▶ Step 3

Listen to two sample responses. Write down any useful expressions. Track 20

Notes

____

____

____

____

____

____

____

____

▶ Step 4

Now create your own response using words and expressions from Steps 1, 2, and 3. Use the prompts below to help you.

The woman is ______________________________. She needs to ______________

______________. The man suggests that ______________________________.

I think ______________________________ is best. Since ______________

______________________________. This could ______________

______________________________. Also, ______________

______________. It ______________________________.

This ______________________________.

▶ Step 5

Read the response you wrote above out loud. Try to read slowly and clearly. Practice saying the whole response several times. Then close your book and say the response without looking at the words.

Q5 Practice 2 – Conversation

Step 1

Listen to a conversation. As you listen, take notes on the problem and the solutions suggested. Track 21

Problem: ______________________________

______________________________.

Solution 1: ______________________________

______________________________.

Solution 2: ______________________________

______________________________.

portion:
a piece of something

trail:
a path or track

sympathize:
to show that you understand someone's problems

anxious:
nervous or uneasy

extra credit:
a task that a student can complete to raise his or her grade

Step 2

Read the prompt below. Write down your opinion.

The students discuss two possible solutions to the man's problem. Describe the problem. Then state which of the two solutions you prefer and explain why.

Problem: ______________________________

Best solution: ______________________________

Reason 1: ______________________________

Reason 2: ______________________________

Step 3

Listen to two sample responses. Write down any useful expressions. Track 22

Notes

____

____

____

____

____

____

____

____

Step 4

Now create your own response using words and expressions from Steps 1, 2, and 3. Use the prompts below to help you.

The man has to ____________________. The trip ____________________. The woman suggests ____________________. I think it would be better ____________________. Since ____________________. Also, ____________________. It is ____________________.

Step 5

Read the response you wrote above out loud. Try to read slowly and clearly. Practice saying the whole response several times. Then close your book and say the response without looking at the words.

Practice 3 – Conversation

▸ Step 1

Listen to a conversation. As you listen, take notes on the problem and the solutions suggested. Track 23

Problem: ______________________________

______________________________.

Solution 1: ______________________________

______________________________.

Solution 2: ______________________________

______________________________.

load:
weight or burden

exchange:
to trade

flexible:
adaptable or able to change easily

loan:
something that has been given with the expectation that it will be returned

debt:
something owed

▸ Step 2

Read the prompt below. Write down your opinion.

The students discuss two possible solutions to the woman's problem. Describe the problem. Then state which of the two solutions you prefer and explain why.

Problem: ______________________________

Best solution: ______________________________

Reason 1: ______________________________

Reason 2: ______________________________

Step 3

Listen to two sample responses. Write down any useful expressions. Track 24

Notes

Step 4

Now create your own response using words and expressions from Steps 1, 2, and 3. Use the prompts below to help you.

The woman ______________________________.

The man suggests ______________________________. It ______________________________. This option ______________________________. She ______________________________. In addition, ______________________________. This way, ______________________________.

Step 5

Read the response you wrote above out loud. Try to read slowly and clearly. Practice saying the whole response several times. Then close your book and say the response without looking at the words.

Q6 Practice 1 – Lecture

Step 1

Listen to a lecture. Fill in the missing information in the notes. Track 25

Minimalism is ____

____

Design techniques used by minimalist artists:

a) ____

b) ____

Carl Andre's "Steel Zinc Plain":

Used the technique of ____

Physical description: ____

Dan Flavin's "Monument for V. Tatlin":

Used the technique of ____

Physical description: ____

prominent: famous or well-known
texture: the feel and appearance of a surface
uniform: unvarying; identical
zinc: a type of metal
checkerboard: a pattern of squares of equal size and of two different colors
interpret: to understand or explain
miniature: small
monument: a structure acting as a memorial
revolving: tending to turn
grandeur: majesty, magnificence or greatness

Step 2

Read the prompt below related to the lecture you heard.

Using points from the lecture, describe two characteristics of minimalist art and give examples of how these characteristics were used to create artwork.

Now create your own response using words and expressions from Step 1. Use the prompts below to help you.

Minimalist artists ____________________. The professor says ____________________ ____________________. The first piece that the professor mentioned ____________________ ____________________. In his piece, ____________________. The second piece ____________________. For his piece, ____________________ ____________________. This ____________________ was inspired ____________________.

Step 3

Listen to a sample response. Write down any useful expressions. Track 26

Notes

Step 4

Review the response you wrote in Step 2 and your notes in Step 3. Then close your book and give a response to the prompt below. Say your response slowly and clearly. Try to speak for at least 60 seconds.

Using points from the lecture, describe two characteristics of minimalist art and give examples of how these characteristics were used to create artwork.

Q6 Practice 2 – Lecture

Step 1

Listen to a lecture. Fill in the missing information in the notes. Track 27

Charisma definition: ______________________________

____

Traits of charismatic leadership:

a) ______________________________

b) ______________________________

Dr. Martin Luther King, Jr.:

He demonstrated ______________________________

His accomplishments: ______________________________

General Patton:

He demonstrated ______________________________

He showed this by ______________________________

attribute: a quality or trait
compelling: convincing or persuasive
vision: an idea or mental picture; a dream
inspire: to motivate or encourage
delegate: to assign or appoint
exhibit: to show or demonstrate
traffic jam: a situation when all traffic is very slow
jeep: a small, sturdy vehicle with 4-wheel drive
subordinate: lower workers or associates
admiration: respect or high regard

Step 2

Read the prompt below related to the lecture you heard.

Using points and examples from the lecture, describe the two traits of a charismatic leader and explain how these traits were used.

Now create your own response using words and expressions from Step 1. Use the prompts below to help you.

The professor ______________________________. One trait of a charismatic leader is ______________________________. The professor uses ______________ as an example ______________. His vision ______________________________. He ______________________________. The second trait of a charismatic leader is ______________________________. The professor uses ______________ as an example. He ______________________________.

Step 3

Listen to a sample response. Write down any useful expressions. Track 28

Notes

Step 4

Review the response you wrote in Step 2 and your notes in Step 3. Then close your book and give a response to the prompt below. Say your response slowly and clearly. Try to speak for at least 60 seconds.

Using points and examples from the lecture, describe the two traits of a charismatic leader and explain how these traits were used.

Q6 Practice 3 – Lecture

Step 1

Listen to a lecture. Fill in the missing information in the notes. Track 29

The Asch experiment revealed ______________________________

____

Description of Asch experiment: ______________________________

____

Response of the last student: ______________________________

____

What Asch believed would happen: ______________________________

____

What actually happened: ______________________________

____

tendency:
likelihood; movement in a given direction

conform:
to agree or match

compromise:
to cooperate or give in

series:
a number of objects or events arranged one after another

ignorant:
unaware

previously:
at an earlier time

sacrifice:
to give up or surrender

crowd:
a large number of people gathered together

contradict:
to disagree with or go against

Step 2

Read the prompt below related to the lecture you heard.

Using points and examples from the lecture, describe Asch's experiment and what it says about conformity.

Now create your own response using words and expressions from Step 1. Use the prompts below to help you.

The professor says ______________________________.

For his experiment, ______________________________. All ______________________________. Asch found ______________________________. Asch's experiment showed ______________________________.

▸ Step 3

Listen to a sample response. Write down any useful expressions. Track 30

Notes

▸ Step 4

Review the response you wrote in Step 2 and your notes in Step 3. Then close your book and give a response to the prompt below. Say your response slowly and clearly. Try to speak for at least 60 seconds.

Using points and examples from the lecture, describe Asch's experiment and what it says about conformity.

Vocabulary Review 1

Instructions: Choose the best word or phrase to complete each sentence.

1. In order to register for my classes, my university gave me a __________ of numbers which would act as my school ID.

(A) portion
(B) series
(C) rank
(D) load

2. I am now attending university in San Francisco. However, I __________ in Tokyo and lived there until recently.

(A) exchanged
(B) accommodated
(C) registered
(D) originated

3. When I become an adult, I would like to live in a(n) __________ climate. I'd particularly like to dwell on a tropical island.

(A) maritime
(B) remote
(C) alpine
(D) molten

4. The rough __________ of this painting made it look as if the artist had hastily put it together.

(A) texture
(B) color spectrum
(C) symbolism
(D) proximity

5. Many people consider certain laws to be __________. All cultures seem to share these laws.

(A) diverse
(B) substantial
(C) universal
(D) distinct

6. Emily printed a first __________ of her research paper for her physics professor to look over. He marked several errors before returning it to her.

(A) journal
(B) catalogue
(C) novel
(D) draft

7. The dog's behavior was very __________ toward me. It made me feel very afraid.

(A) dominant
(B) anxious
(C) menacing
(D) overwhelming

8. Jason's computer was malfunctioning. It would not let him __________ his personal files.

(A) log
(B) access
(C) flip
(D) navigate

Instructions: Choose the word or phrase closest in meaning to the underlined word.

9. The lemurs, types of monkeys from Madagascar, are becoming endangered because their <u>homes</u> are being destroyed.

(A) habitats
(B) continents
(C) summits
(D) savannas

10. The mother decided to let her daughter <u>recover</u> from her recent cold by allowing her to stay home from school.

(A) drift
(B) sympathize
(C) induce
(D) recuperate

11. Although I had studied hard the night before, I felt so apprehensive about the test that I nearly made myself sick.

(A) exhausted
(B) anxious
(C) relaxed
(D) flexible

12. As manager of this photography studio, I try to treat my workers with the utmost respect.

(A) photographers
(B) consultants
(C) subordinates
(D) authorities

13. Despite the fact that I didn't agree with him, I found his argument to be very persuasive.

(A) compelling
(B) inconvenient
(C) relaxed
(D) prominent

14. I received the money that I needed on credit, but I'll have to pay it back later.

(A) fundraiser
(B) load
(C) debt
(D) loan

15. My sister decided to help others by volunteering at the local charity.

(A) hang out with
(B) date back to
(C) reach out to
(D) hang up on

Instructions: Write the missing words. Use the words below to fill in the blanks.

penalty	afford	ignorant
scholarship	unscholarly	

One bad event that taught me a lesson happened last year. I couldn't **16.** ________________ to pay for college anymore, so I had applied for and won a **17.** ________________. Yet I was **18.** ________________ of its conditions. The next semester, I took a physical education class for fun. However, the terms of my scholarship stated that I could not take any class that was **19.** ________________ in nature. Hence, I almost lost it because I did not read the terms carefully enough. That would have been a severe **20.** ________________ for such a simple mistake.

Instructions: Match the words that have opposite meanings.

21. current	(A) ally
22. ancestor	(B) plenty
23. scarce	(C) nearby
24. opponent	(D) dated
25. isolated	(E) descendent

Vocabulary Review 2

Instructions: Choose the best word or phrase to complete each sentence.

1. Susie got a prescription for medication from her medical doctor, but she decided that she would wait to __________ her therapist before she took any new pills.
   (A) obtain
   (B) consult
   (C) ace
   (D) chat

2. My teacher resolved a recent __________ between myself and a friend.
   (A) opponent
   (B) debt
   (C) conflict
   (D) hassle

3. In the mountains close to my house, there is a large __________ of the rock, granite.
   (A) trail
   (B) zinc
   (C) attribute
   (D) deposit

4. I needed to make a(n) __________ stop at the nearest car repair shop because my tire had blown out.
   (A) firsthand
   (B) emergency
   (C) overdue
   (D) monetary

5. The actor's compassionate actions __________ me to participate more in improving my own community.
   (A) enabled
   (B) deterred
   (C) inspired
   (D) evoked

6. George could speak Italian fluently, but he was still unable to __________ what the plot of the opera was about.
   (A) post
   (B) enable
   (C) devise
   (D) interpret

7. Her high-school science project had been so __________ for Cynthia that it nearly brought her to tears.
   (A) overwhelming
   (B) exhausted
   (C) anxious
   (D) remarkable

8. On Monday, I need to visit the __________ office to get a list of my previous classes.
   (A) transcript's
   (B) security's
   (C) registrar's
   (D) network's

Instructions: Choose the word closest in meaning to the underlined word or phrase.

9. Whenever I stop by the store, I prefer to buy <u>natural</u> food over food with lots of added preservatives.
   (A) prominent
   (B) organic
   (C) substantial
   (D) current

10. The <u>outer covering</u> of the Earth covers the liquid mantle that exists below the Earth.
    (A) deposit
    (B) fossil
    (C) continent
    (D) crust

11. The mother tried to split her time evenly between her three-year-old and her newborn.

(A) vary
(B) waste
(C) divide
(D) exhibit

12. Even though the appointment was time-consuming and very problematic, I was happy to get it over with.

(A) prominent
(B) inconvenient
(C) flexible
(D) scarce

13. The scientist came up with a solid premise to explain the observations he had witnessed.

(A) hypothesis
(B) allocation
(C) goal
(D) vision

14. Since they couldn't agree on which restaurant to eat at, my parents decided to negotiate by selecting a third restaurant choice.

(A) sacrifice
(B) compromise
(C) conform
(D) contradict

15. The small building that the architect constructed was modeled after its larger counterpart.

(A) diverse
(B) universal
(C) miniature
(D) revolving

Instructions: Write the missing words. Use the words below to fill in the blanks.

endures	grandeur	remarkable
traffic jam	monument	

My favorite vacation was when my family and I went to visit Mount Rushmore, a **16.** ________________ in the United States. It was hard to get there at first because our vehicle got stuck in a **17.** ________________. However, when we finally got there, I was amazed by the **18.** ________________ of the site. It was **19.** ________________ to see the large heads of past American presidents carved out in stone. Best of all, this site **20.** ________________ rain, snow, and the tests of time, which allows people like me to see it in the future.

Instructions: Choose one word in each group that does not belong.

21. contend, assert, insist, rebuke

22. admiration, esteem, dejection, veneration

23. uniform, varied, identical, equal

24. assume, delegate, assign, allocate

25. previously, subsequently, prior to, formerly

Part 2

Making Speech Coherent

- **Chapter 4** **Independent Speaking: Test Questions 1 and 2**
- **Chapter 5** **Integrated Speaking: Test Questions 3 and 4**
- **Chapter 6** **Integrated Speaking: Test Questions 5 and 6**
- **Vocabulary Review 3**
- **Vocabulary Review 4**

Chapter 4 Independent Speaking: Test Questions 1 and 2

A response to the independent speaking question generally includes the following:

- An introduction to the general topic of the essay — usually one sentence
- A statement of your opinion — usually one sentence
- Your reasons + examples/details to support them — one or two sentences each

Within 60 seconds, the time given for your response, you should be able to say about eight sentences. These sentences would be similar in length to the following: "I often take my guitar to parties and play music for my friends there."

Before speaking:

- Choose an opinion that is easily supported.
- Organize the flow of your response in your mind.
- Make sure that you have adequate reasons and examples.

When speaking:

- Make a clear statement of your opinion on the given topic.
- State clear reasons for your opinion.
- Use concrete examples.
- Use transitions to improve the flow of your speech.

Chapter 4

Q1 Practice 1 – Personal Experience

Step 1

Read and think about the prompt below.

Where is your favorite place to go in your city? Why do you enjoy going there? Include specific reasons and examples to support your answer.

The sentences below make up a response to the prompt above. Read the sentences and underline any transitions you find.

(A) For instance, I can watch people jogging, couples walking their dogs, or children playing at the playground.
(B) This game is a great way to meet new friends, get some exercise, and take a break from schoolwork.
(C) My favorite place to go to in my city is the huge park downtown.
(D) It is fun to see how they all interact with each other.
(E) I love going there because it is a great place to watch people doing various activities.
(F) Also, I enjoy going to the park because I can almost always find someone to play volleyball with.

downtown:
the central part of a city that usually consists of the business center
various:
of different kinds
jog:
to run at a steady pace
playground:
an outdoor area set up for children to play
volleyball:
a game played by two teams where a ball is hit over a net

Look at the sentences again. Think about the role of each sentence in the response. Then list the sentences in the correct order.

▸ Step 2

Do NOT look at the sentences in Step 1. Answer the following questions in complete sentences.

1. Where is this person's favorite place?

____

2. What does she like to do there?

____

3. Why does she choose to do these activities there?

____

Using the answers you wrote above, try to speak for 60 seconds explaining this person's response. Use the words and phrases below while you are speaking. Record your time.

for instance	also	favorite place	always	enjoy	fun

Response 1: Speaking time: ____________ seconds

▸ Step 3

Now listen to the sample response. How is it different from yours? What parts of the response can you use in your own? Write down any helpful expressions you hear. Track 31

Notes

____

____

____

____

Listen again and repeat after the response. Pay close attention to pronunciation, intonation, and word stress. Track 32

▸ Step 4

Now write your own answers to the following questions in complete sentences.

1. Where is your favorite place to go in your city?

____

2. What activities do you like to do there?

____

3. Why do you choose to do these activities there?

____

Using the short answers you wrote above, give a spoken response to the prompt. Try to incorporate useful expressions from Step 3, while also paying attention to your pronunciation and intonation. Record your time.

> Where is your favorite place to go in your city? Why do you enjoy going there? Include specific reasons and examples to support your answer.

Response 2: Speaking time: ____________ seconds

Q1 Practice 2 – Personal Experience

▸ Step 1

Read and think about the prompt below.

> Describe a favorite book that you read as a child. Why did you like it so much? Include specific reasons and examples to support your answer.

The sentences below make up a response to the prompt above. Read the sentences and underline any transitions you find.

(A) I liked the book mostly because of its great pictures.
(B) I felt proud because I could recite the story even before I knew how to read.
(C) Even though the Wild Things are supposed to be fearsome monsters, they are actually quite comical in the pictures.
(D) It is about a boy who uses his imagination to turn his room into a wild forest where he becomes the king of the Wild Things.
(E) I also liked the book because the story was simple and easy to memorize.
(F) As a child, one of my favorite books was *Where the Wild Things Are*.

imagination: ability to think of intelligent and original ideas or thoughts
memorize: to learn something so that you can remember it completely
fearsome: alarming or terrible
comical: funny
recite: to repeat or perform a piece of writing

Look at the sentences again. Think about the role of each sentence in the response. Then list the sentences in the correct order.

____ ▸ ____ ▸ ____ ▸ ____ ▸ ____ ▸ ____

Step 2

Do NOT look at the sentences in Step 1. Answer the following questions in complete sentences.

1. What was this person's favorite book about?

____

2. Why did he like this book as a child?

____

3. What was surprising about the monsters in the story?

____

Using the answers you wrote above, try to speak for 60 seconds explaining this person's response. Use the words and phrases below while you are speaking. Record your time.

as a child	even though	also	like	mostly	favorite	because

Response 1: Speaking time: ____________ seconds

Step 3

Now listen to the sample response. How is it different from yours? What parts of the response can you use in your own? Write down any helpful expressions you hear. Track 33

Notes

Listen again and repeat after the response. Pay close attention to pronunciation, intonation, and word stress. Track 34

Step 4

Now write your own answers to the following questions in complete sentences.

1. What was your favorite book about?

____

2. Why did you like this book as a child?

____

3. What was surprising about the book?

____

Using the answers you wrote above, give a spoken response to the prompt. Try to incorporate useful expressions from Step 3, while also paying attention to your pronunciation and intonation. Record your time.

> Describe a favorite book that you read as a child. Why did you like it so much? Include specific reasons and examples to support your answer.

Response 2: Speaking time: ____________ seconds

Q1 Practice 3 – Personal Experience

▸ Step 1

Read and think about the prompt below.

Describe a teacher who has positively impacted your life. How has he or she influenced you? Include specific reasons and examples to support your answer.

A sample outline of a response is given below. Write down transition words or phrases that can be used to link the ideas.

Teacher: Ms. Murphy, 9th grade

- Reason 1: Helped me develop a passion for literature
- Reason 2: Taught me how to deal with conflicts

Transition words/phrases:

__________ __________

__________ __________

__________ __________

Using the above outline, give a spoken response to the prompt. Record your time.

Response 1: Speaking time: __________ seconds

▸ Step 2

Now listen to the sample response. How is it different from yours? What parts of the response can you use in your own? Write down any helpful expressions you hear. Track 35

Notes

____

____

____

____

____

impact:
to influence

passion:
love and enthusiasm for something

pursue:
to follow or go after

rationally:
sensibly, reasonably

temper:
a state of calm and balance

Listen again and repeat after the response. Pay close attention to pronunciation, intonation, and word stress. Track 36

▸ Step 3

Without listening to the sample again, give another spoken response to the prompt. Try to incorporate useful expressions from Step 2, while also paying attention to your pronunciation and intonation. Record your time.

Response 2: Speaking time: ____________ seconds

▸ Step 4

Make your own outline for the prompt. Try to incorporate transition words and useful phrases introduced in Steps 1 and 2.

Teacher: ______________________________

- Reason 1: ______________________________

  ____

- Reason 2: ______________________________

  ____

Transition words/phrases:

____________	____________
____________	____________
____________	____________

Using your outline, respond to the prompt. Record your time.

Describe a teacher who has positively impacted your life. How has he or she influenced you? Include specific reasons and examples to support your answer.

Response 3: Speaking time: ____________ seconds

Q1 Practice 4 – Personal Experience

Step 1

Read and think about the prompt below.

> Who has given you good advice and what was it? Why was this good advice? Include specific reasons and examples to support your answer.

A sample outline of a response is given below. Write down transition words or phrases that can be used to link the ideas.

Mother's advice: Focus on schoolwork

- Reason 1: Received high grades
  Detail: Earned a college scholarship
- Reason 2: Allowed me to graduate at the top of my class
  Detail: Eligible for many jobs

Transition words/phrases:

_____________ _____________

_____________ _____________

_____________ _____________

Using the above outline, give a spoken response to the prompt. Record your time.

Response 1: Speaking time: _____________ seconds

Step 2

Now listen to the sample response. How is it different from yours? What parts of the response can you use in your own? Write down any helpful expressions you hear. Track 37

Notes

____

____

____

____

____

concentrate: to think; to focus

acquire: to obtain or possess

eventually: finally or ultimately

habit: a routine or custom

eligible: qualified for

Listen again and repeat after the response. Pay close attention to pronunciation, intonation, and word stress. Track 38

▸ Step 3

Without listening to the sample again, give another spoken response to the prompt. Try to incorporate useful expressions from Step 2, while also paying attention to your pronunciation and intonation. Record your time.

Response 2: Speaking time: ____________ seconds

▸ Step 4

Make your own outline for the prompt. Try to incorporate transition words and useful phrases introduced in Steps 1 and 2.

____________ **advice:** ____________________

____

- Reason 1: ________________________________

____

Detail: __________________________________

____

- Reason 2: ________________________________

____

Detail: __________________________________

____

Transition words/phrases:

____________ ____________

____________ ____________

____________ ____________

Using your outline, respond to the prompt. Record your time.

> Who has given you good advice and what was it? Why was this good advice? Include specific reasons and examples to support your answer.

Response 3: Speaking time: ____________ seconds

Q2 Practice 1 – Personal Preference

▸ Step 1

Read and think about the prompt below.

> Some students prefer to attend prestigious national universities. Others prefer to attend local colleges. Which would you prefer and why? Use specific reasons and examples to support your answer.

The sentences below make up a response to the prompt above. Read the sentences and underline any transitions you find.

(A) In high school, when I was doing poorly in a class, they were there to give me the advice I needed to pass it.
(B) I know many graduates of less expensive local colleges who have attained even more success than those from prestigious universities.
(C) Secondly, I think I would receive as good an education at a local college as at a national college, and at half the cost.
(D) This way, if I encountered any problems, my family would be nearby to provide assistance.
(E) I would prefer to attend a local college.
(F) I would also want their support in college.

local: nearby; close to home
encounter: to meet or come across
assistance: help; aid
attain: achieve; accomplish
prestigious: high-status

Look at the sentences again. Think about the role of each sentence in the response. Then list the sentences in the correct order.

▸ Step 2

Do NOT look at the sentences in Step 1. Answer the following questions in complete sentences.

1. Which type of college or university does this person wish to attend?

____

2. What is one reason she gives for holding this opinion?

____

3. What is another reason she gives for holding this opinion?

____

Using the short answers you wrote above, try to speak for 60 seconds explaining this person's response. Use the words and phrases below, while you are speaking. Record your time.

also	prefer	prestigious	local	secondly	college	this way

Response 1: Speaking time: ____________ seconds

▸ Step 3

Now listen to the sample response. How is it different from yours? What parts of the response can you use in your own? Write down any helpful expressions you hear. Track 39

Notes

____

____

____

____

Listen again and repeat after the response. Pay close attention to pronunciation, intonation, and word stress. Track 40

▸ Step 4

Now write your own answers to the following questions in complete sentences.

1. Which type of college or university would you like to attend?

___

2. What is one reason you have for holding this opinion?

___

3. What is another reason you have for holding this opinion?

___

Using the short answers you wrote above, give a spoken response to the prompt. Try to incorporate useful expressions from Step 3, while also paying attention to your pronunciation and intonation. Record your time.

> Some students prefer to attend prestigious national universities. Others prefer to attend local colleges. Which would you prefer and why? Include specific reasons and examples to support your answer.

Response 2: Speaking time: ______________ seconds

Practice 2 – Personal Preference

Step 1

Read and think about the prompt below.

> When some people travel to new areas, they like to visit educational places like museums. Others prefer to spend time at more entertaining places like amusement parks. Which do you prefer and why? Include specific reasons and examples to support your answer.

The sentences below make up a response to the prompt above. Read the sentences and underline any transitions you find.

(A) Since I can visit places like those at home, I would rather spend my time at places I will not see again.
(B) I also enjoy visiting educational places because they are often distinctive to an area.
(C) Primarily, I like visiting educational places like museums because I am often curious about the area and the people I am visiting.
(D) In contrast, places for entertainment like movie theaters or amusement parks can generally be found anywhere.
(E) I prefer to visit educational places when I travel to new areas.
(F) I think that knowing the history and culture of a place helps me to better understand and appreciate it.

primarily:
mainly; chiefly
museum:
a building where valuable objects are kept so that people can see them
curious:
eager to learn
distinctive:
specific to a certain place
generally:
usually or normally

Look at the sentences again. Think about the role of each sentence in the response. Then list the sentences in the correct order.

▸ Step 2

Do NOT look at the sentences in Step 1. Answer the following questions in complete sentences.

1. Which type of place does this person prefer to visit?

   ____

2. What is the first reason he gives for his preference?

   ____

3. What does he say is a major difference between educational places and places devoted solely to entertainment?

   ____

Using the short answers you wrote above, try to speak for 60 seconds explaining this person's response. Use the words and phrases below, while you are speaking. Record your time.

since	also	in contrast	primarily	educational	entertainment

Response 1: Speaking time: __________ seconds

▸ Step 3

Now listen to the sample response. How is it different from yours? What parts of the response can you use in your own? Write down any helpful expressions you hear. Track 41

Notes

____

____

____

____

Listen again and repeat after the response. Pay close attention to pronunciation, intonation, and word stress. Track 42

Step 4

Now write your own answers to the following questions in complete sentences.

1. Which type of place would you prefer to visit?

   ____

2. What is the first reason you would give for your preference?

   ____

3. In your opinion, what is one major difference between educational places and places devoted solely to entertainment?

   ____

Using the short answers you wrote above, give a spoken response to the prompt. Try to incorporate useful expressions from Step 3, while also paying attention to your pronunciation and intonation. Record your time.

> When some people travel to new areas, they like to visit educational places like museums. Others prefer to spend time at more entertaining places like amusement parks. Which do you prefer and why? Include specific reasons and examples to support your answer.

Response 2: Speaking time: ____________ seconds

Practice 3 – Personal Preference

▶ Step 1

Read and think about the prompt below.

> Some people believe that learning material should be the sole responsibility of teachers. Others feel that parents should be involved in choosing the material children learn in school. Which view do you believe? Include specific reasons and examples to support your answer.

A sample outline of a response is given below. Write down transition words or phrases that can be used to link the ideas.

Should parents influence curriculum? Yes

- Reason 1: Parents know best what their children are ready to learn.
- Reason 2: The opinions of parents can be helpful in developing a curriculum.
- Reason 3: Parents can speak for their children when their children are having problems.

Transition words/phrases:

____________ ____________

____________ ____________

____________ ____________

Using the above outline, give a spoken response to the prompt. Record your time.

Response 1: Speaking time: ____________ seconds

▶ Step 2

Now listen to the sample response. How is it different from yours? What parts of the response can you use in your own? Write down any helpful expressions you hear. Track 43

Notes

____

____

____

____

____

firmly:
confidently; resistant to pressure

judge:
one who evaluates

struggle:
to have trouble with

curriculum:
the courses of study offered by an institution

intervene:
to interfere or get involved in

Listen again and repeat after the response. Pay close attention to pronunciation, intonation, and word stress. Track 44

Step 3

Without listening to the sample again, give another spoken response to the prompt. Try to incorporate useful expressions from Step 2, while also paying attention to your pronunciation and intonation. Record your time.

Response 2: Speaking time: ____________ seconds

Step 4

Make your own outline for the prompt. Try to incorporate transition words and useful phrases introduced in Steps 1 and 2.

Should parents influence curriculum? ______

- Reason 1: ______________________________
  ____
- Reason 2: ______________________________
  ____
- Reason 3: ______________________________
  ____

Transition words/phrases:

__________ __________
__________ __________
__________ __________

Using your outline, respond to the prompt. Record your time.

> Some people believe that learning material should be the sole responsibility of teachers. Others feel that parents should be involved in choosing the material children learn in school. Which view do you believe? Include specific reasons and examples to support your answer.

Response 3: Speaking time: ____________ seconds

Practice 4 – Personal Preference

Step 1

Read and think about the prompt below.

In today's busy world, people are constantly on the move. Many prefer this active lifestyle because they feel it is more exciting. Do you think it is a good idea to be constantly active? Include specific reasons and examples to support your answer.

A sample outline of a response is given below. Write down transition words or phrases that can be used to link the ideas.

Is it good to be constantly active? No

- Reason 1: Too much activity drains us of energy.
- Reason 2: Bodies need rest to function properly.
- Reason 3: It is more efficient to take breaks between activities.

Transition words/phrases:

_______________ _______________

_______________ _______________

_______________ _______________

Using the above outline, give a spoken response to the prompt. Record your time.

Response 1: Speaking time: _______________ seconds

Step 2

Now listen to the sample response. How is it different from yours? What parts of the response can you use in your own? Write down any helpful expressions you hear. Track 45

Notes

drain:
to use up or exhaust

recharge:
to renew or refresh

counterproductive:
making something worse rather than better

efficiently:
to do well or capably

break:
a pause in work

Listen again and repeat after the response. Pay close attention to pronunciation, intonation, and word stress. Track 46

▶ Step 3

Without listening to the sample again, give another spoken response to the prompt. Try to incorporate useful expressions from Step 2, while also paying attention to your pronunciation and intonation. Record your time.

Response 2: Speaking time: ____________ seconds

▶ Step 4

Make your own outline for the prompt. Try to incorporate transition words and useful phrases introduced in Steps 1 and 2.

Is it good to be constantly active? ____________

- Reason 1: ______________________________
  ____
- Reason 2: ______________________________
  ____
- Reason 3: ______________________________
  ____

Transition words/phrases:

__________ __________
__________ __________
__________ __________

Using your outline, respond to the prompt. Record your time.

In today's busy world, people are constantly on the move. Many prefer this active lifestyle because they feel it is more exciting. Do you think it is a good idea to be constantly active? Use specific reasons and examples to support your answer.

Response 3: Speaking time: ____________ seconds

Chapter 5 Integrated Speaking: Test Questions 3 and 4

A response to the integrated speaking questions generally includes the following:

Question 3

- A statement of the problem or situation, as expressed in the reading
- A statement of the speaker's opinion, as introduced in the conversation
- His or her reasons + additional information, as taken from the conversation

Question 4

- A statement of the main idea or topic of the reading and lecture
- Key points that are similar
- Key points that contrast

Before speaking:

- Identify the topic and supporting details.
- Organize the flow of your response in your mind.
- Make sure that you have adequate reasons and examples.

While speaking:

- Begin your response by clearly stating the opinion / main idea of the reading and the conversation/lecture.
- Give reasons or details from the conversation or lecture to support your opinion.
- Make sure statements are clearly connected so that the scorer will more easily understand your points.

Q3 Practice 1 – Reading and Conversation

Step 1

Read the passage below and underline important information.

Attention Honors Students

The English Department is now making it mandatory for all honors students who are planning to attend graduate school to take pre-graduate classes offered by the English Department. For those of you who are planning on pursuing a master's or doctoral degree, these classes are designed specifically to prepare you for graduate courses. They will facilitate the transition from college to graduate education. These high-level courses will also allow your graduate school application to stand out from among a pool of applicants from other schools.

mandatory: required; compulsory
doctoral: relating to the highest academic degree
specifically: particularly or expressly
facilitate: to assist or to make easy
transition: a change in state
pool: a joint supply that is used by members of a group

Write down the main idea and any key points.

Notes

____

____

____

____

Now listen to a related conversation. Take notes on the woman's opinion. Track 47

Opinion: ______________________________

Reason 1: ______________________________

____

Reason 2: ______________________________

____

policy: procedure
bet: to think or expect
excel: to do well
competitive: relating to competition
applicant: someone that applies for something

▶ Step 2

Read and think about the prompt below.

> The woman expresses her opinion of the English Department's decision. State her opinion and explain the reasons she gives for holding that opinion.

WITHOUT looking at the original reading passage, review your notes from the reading and listening passages. Select the information you think is important. Fill in the blanks of the sample response below.

The announcement says ____.

The woman __________ with this idea. She says that ______________________________

______________________________. ______________________________.

She supports this point ____.

She thinks ______________________________________. Also, ______________

______________________________________. She says that ______________

______________________________________.

After you have filled in the blanks, read the response out loud. Pay attention to your pronunciation, intonation, and word stress.

Step 3

Now listen to a sample response. How does it differ from your response? Write down any differences in information or phrasing. Track 48

Notes

Listen again and repeat after the response. Pay close attention to pronunciation, intonation, and word stress. Track 49

Step 4

Now give your own spoken response to the prompt. Try to incorporate useful expressions from Steps 2 and 3, while also paying attention to your pronunciation and intonation. Record your time.

Response: Speaking time: ______________ seconds

Practice 2 – Reading and Conversation

Step 1

Read the passage below and underline important information.

Announcement

All counselors at the Business School will now have open office hours at three specified times during the week to talk with students and answer questions. In the past, students have had to schedule counseling appointments weeks in advance and have consequently been unable to get their questions answered in a timely manner. Additionally, we often did not have enough counselors available during the whole week to handle student demand. We expect that by providing open office hours, students can get answers to questions quickly and there will be enough counselors available during these times to meet the demand.

in advance: beforehand or prior to
counselor: a person who provides advice and assistance to students at an institution
timely: occurring at a suitable time
manner: method or way
available: at hand; able to be obtained

Write down the main idea and any key points.

Notes

____

____

____

____

Now listen to a related conversation. Take notes on the man's opinion. Track 50

Opinion: ________________________

Reason 1: He often has trouble ________________________

Example: ________________________

Reason 2: His questions ________________________

Example: ________________________

bulletin: a brief report or announcement
news: new information about recent events
exasperating: annoying or irritating
issue: a subject or topic
show up: to come or attend
precisely: exactly

▸ Step 2

Read and think about the prompt below.

> The man expresses his opinion of the university's decision. State his opinion and explain the reasons he gives for holding that opinion.

WITHOUT looking at the original reading passage, review your notes from the reading and listening passages. Select the information you think is important. Fill in the blanks of the sample response below.

The announcement says ____

______________________________. The man thinks ______________________________

_______________. He ____.

He also ____.

Most counselors ________________________________. Therefore, ________________.

Now, according to the man, ____. Since

____.

After you have filled in the blanks, read the response out loud. Pay attention to your pronunciation, intonation, and word stress.

Step 3

Now listen to a sample response. How does it differ from your response? Write down any differences in information or phrasing. Track 51

Notes

Listen again and repeat after the response. Pay close attention to pronunciation, intonation, and word stress. Track 52

Step 4

Now give your own spoken response to the prompt. Try to incorporate useful expressions from Steps 2 and 3, while also paying attention to your pronunciation and intonation. Record your time.

Response: Speaking time: ____________ seconds

Practice 1 – Reading and Lecture

Step 1

Read the passage below and underline important information.

Ways the Brain Can Recover from Damage

Neuroscientists have often observed that children who have suffered from severe brain damage can sometimes miraculously recover much of the brain's functions. Adults have a harder time recovering from similar brain damage because once the brain stops developing, it becomes hard-wired. Neuroscientists used to believe that brain damage was permanent in adults.

However, neuroscientists now think that adults who have severe brain damage can recover brain functions that were once thought to be lost. According to this theory, parts of the adult brain can sometimes create new brain cells. In addition, the brain can also partially recover by adapting to take on new functions.

neuroscientist:
an individual who studies the nervous system, including the brain

hard-wired:
fixed or unchangeable

permanent:
something that lasts forever

cell:
the smallest structural unit of an organism

adapt:
to change or alter

Write down the main idea and any key points.

Notes

____

____

____

____

Now listen to a related lecture. Fill in the missing information. Track 53

Ways the Adult Brain ______________________

Way 1: ______________________

How this happens: ______________________

How this was discovered: ______________________

Way 2: ______________________

How this happens: ______________________

Example: ______________________

tissue:
a collection of similar cells working together to form specific functions within the body

regenerate:
to form or create new things

degree:
level or amount

task:
a job or a piece of work

stroke:
an injury to the brain that happens when inadequate blood flow causes the death of brain cells

motor:
related to movement

▸ Step 2

Read and think about the prompt below.

> The professor discusses two ways the brain can recover from brain damage. Explain what they are and how they occur.

WITHOUT looking at the original reading passage, review your notes from the reading and listening passages. Select the information you think is important. Fill in the blanks of the sample response below.

According to the reading, ____

________________. The professor explains ____.

She says ____. She says __________

____. She then explains________________________

____. The professor gives ____________________

__________________________________. Sometimes ____________________________________

_________. They ____.

After you have filled in the blanks, read the response out loud. Pay attention to your pronunciation, intonation, and word stress.

Step 3

Now listen to a sample response. How does it differ from your response? Write down any differences in information or phrasing. Track 54

Notes

Listen again and repeat after the response. Pay close attention to pronunciation, intonation, and word stress. Track 55

Step 4

Now give your own spoken response to the prompt. Try to incorporate useful expressions from Steps 2 and 3, while also paying attention to your pronunciation and intonation. Record your time.

Response: Speaking time: _______________ seconds

Practice 2 – Reading and Lecture

Step 1

Read the passage below and underline important information.

Interactive Television

Interactive television has many negative effects on today's children. Interactive television involves a variety of systems that allow viewers to interact with television content as they view it. For children, interactive television systems are usually designed with an educational component in mind. Such systems come with a controller by which a child can manipulate the games and videos playing on a television screen. However, researchers are now theorizing that interactive television can negatively affect intelligence in children. Moreover, interactive television can also allow companies to target children for non-educational purposes.

content: materials
component: factor or feature
manipulate: to influence or control
theorize: to come up with a theory; to guess
target: to aim or pursue

Write down the main idea and any key points.

Notes

____

____

____

____

Now listen to a related lecture. Fill in the missing information.

Track 56

Negative Effects of ______________________________

Effect 1: ______________________________

Study 1: ______________________________

Study 2: ______________________________

Effect 2: ______________________________

How this happens: ______________________________

Why this is a problem: ______________________________

cognitively: relating to mental awareness and perception
toddler: a young child learning to walk; a child under age two
beverage: a liquid used for drinking
inherently: an essential characteristic or something that occurs naturally
vulnerable: weak or defenseless
gender: identity based on sex

▸ Step 2

Read and think about the prompt below.

> The professor discusses interactive television. Explain what this is and how it can have a negative effect on children.

WITHOUT looking at the original reading passage, review your notes from the reading and listening passages. Select the information you think is important. Fill in the blanks of the sample response below.

According to the reading, ____

_______. The professor expands on this first point ______________________________

____. Tests ___________

____. Yet __________________________.

He also says ____

___________. They can ____.

Children ____.

After you have filled in the blanks, read the response out loud. Pay attention to your pronunciation, intonation, and word stress.

Step 3

Now listen to a sample response. How does it differ from your response? Write down any differences in information or phrasing. Track 57

Notes

Listen again and repeat after the response. Pay close attention to pronunciation, intonation, and word stress. Track 58

Step 4

Now give your own spoken response to the prompt. Try to incorporate useful expressions from Steps 2 and 3, while also paying attention to your pronunciation and intonation. Record your time.

Response: Speaking time: ____________ seconds

Chapter 6 Integrated Speaking: Test Questions 5 and 6

A response to the integrated speaking questions generally includes the following:

- A statement of the problem or situation, as expressed in the conversation
- A statement of suggested solutions, as mentioned in the conversation
- An opinion of the suggested solutions
- Reasons + examples and details to support them
- A summary of the main points of the lecture

Before speaking:

- Choose the opinion most easily supported.
- Organize the flow of your answer in your mind.
- Make sure that you have adequate reasons and examples.

When speaking:

- Make a clear statement of your opinion on the given topic.
- State clear reasons for your opinion.
- Use concrete examples.
- Use transitions to improve the flow of your speech.

To describe problems:

- She/He is having a problem with ______________.
- The problem is ______________.
- She/He needs help with ______________.
- She/He is having trouble ______________.
- She/He cannot figure out ______________.

To present opinions/solutions:

- She/He needs to ______________.
- She/He should ______________.
- One (Another) thing she/he can do is ______________.
- The best thing she/he can do is ______________.
- If I were her/him, I would ______________.

Q5 Practice 1 – Conversation

Step 1

Listen to a conversation. Take notes on the problem presented and the possible solutions suggested. Track 59

Problem: ______________________________

Solution 1: ______________________________

Advantages: ______________________________

____

Disadvantages: ______________________________

Solution 2: ______________________________

Advantages: ______________________________

____

Disadvantages: ______________________________

lab:
short for laboratory; a place or room dedicated to scientific research and experimentation

data:
factual information

suggestion:
a proposal or idea

occupied:
busy or engaged

converse:
to talk or communicate

clarify:
to explain

On your own, think of some possible benefits to each solution suggested in the conversation. Write them in the extra spaces provided above.

Step 2

Read and think about the prompt below. Answer the following questions in complete sentences.

The students discuss two possible solutions to the man's problem. Describe the problem. Then state which of the two solutions you prefer and explain why.

1. What is the problem?

____

2. What should the man do?

____

3. Why?

____

Step 3

Now create your own response to this topic using words and expressions from Steps 1 and 2.

The man wants ______________________. However, ______________________ ______________________. The woman suggests ______________________ ______________________. I think ______________________ ______________________. His professor ______________________. I am sure ______________________. Also, ______________________ ______________________. He will ______________________ ______________________.

Now listen to a sample response. How does it differ from your response? Write down any differences in information or phrasing. Track 60

Notes

Listen again and repeat after the response. Pay close attention to pronunciation, intonation, and word stress. Track 61

Step 4

Now give your own spoken response to the prompt. Try to incorporate useful expressions from Step 3, while also paying attention to your pronunciation and intonation. Record your time.

Response: Speaking time: __________ seconds

Q5 Practice 2 – Conversation

Step 1

Listen to a conversation. Take notes on the problem presented and the possible solutions suggested. Track 62

Problem: ______________________________

Solution 1: ______________________________

Advantages: ______________________________

____

Disadvantages: ______________________________

Solution 2: ______________________________

Advantages: ______________________________

____

Disadvantages: ______________________________

enroll:
to register or sign up for something

uneasy:
worried or anxious

campus:
the grounds of an institution, usually a school

escort:
a person accompanying someone as a guard or guide

awkward:
uncomfortable

security guard:
a guard who keeps watch over something

several:
more than a few

park:
to put or leave a vehicle in a certain location

On your own, think of some possible benefits to each solution suggested in the conversation. Write them in the extra spaces provided above.

Step 2

Read and think about the prompt below. Answer the following questions in complete sentences.

> The students discuss two possible solutions to the woman's problem. Describe the problem. Then state which of the two solutions you prefer and explain why.

1. What is the problem?

____

2. What should the woman do?

____

3. Why?

____

▸ Step 3

Now create your own response to this topic using words and expressions from Steps 1 and 2.

The woman wants ______________________________. However, __________ ______________________________. The man suggests ______________________________ ______________________________. I think ______________________________ ______________________________. That way, ______________________________ ______________________________. Also, ______________________________ ______________________________.

Now listen to a sample response. How does it differ from your response? Write down any differences in information or phrasing. Track 63

Notes

____

____

____

____

Listen again and repeat after the response. Pay close attention to pronunciation, intonation, and word stress. Track 64

▸ Step 4

Now give your own spoken response to the prompt. Try to incorporate useful expressions from Step 3, while also paying attention to your pronunciation and intonation. Record your time.

Response: Speaking time: ______________ seconds

Q6 Practice 1 – Lecture

Step 1

Listen to a lecture. Take notes on the information presented. Track 65

Main topic: ____________________

Shared characteristic of the aristocratic hero: ____________________

____

Example 1: ____________________

Details: ____________________

____

Example 2: ____________________

Details: ____________________

____

hero:
a character in a story that has great strength and courage

noble:
royal; someone from the upper class

aristocratic:
someone from the upper class

portray:
to show

legendary:
famous or renowned

reclaim:
to get back or regain

trial:
a test or a hardship

drastically:
significantly; considerably

literary:
relating to literature

comedy:
a work that is humorous and that has a happy ending

Step 2

Read and think about the prompt below. Answer the following questions in complete sentences.

Using points and examples from the lecture, describe the aristocratic hero of Classicism and explain its use in classical literature.

1. What characteristic did all classical heroes share?

____

2. What does the speaker mention about the Greek gods in ancient Greek literature?

____

3. What is one characteristic that is rarely seen in Shakespeare's heroes?

____

Step 3

Now create your own response to this topic using words and expressions from Steps 1 and 2.

The professor says ______________________________

__________. This ____________________. The professor says ____________________.

She mentions ______________________________. He is __________

____________________. The professor mentions ______________________________

______________. The professor then says ______________________________.

She mentions ______________________________.

Even ______________________________.

Now listen to a sample response. How does it differ from your response? Write down any differences in information or phrasing. Track 66

Notes

Listen again and repeat after the response. Pay close attention to pronunciation, intonation, and word stress. Track 67

Step 4

Now give your own spoken response to the prompt. Try to incorporate useful expressions from Step 3, while also paying attention to your pronunciation and intonation. Record your time.

Response: Speaking time: ______________ seconds

Q6 Practice 2 – Lecture

Step 1

Listen to a lecture. Take notes on the information presented. Track 68

Main topic: ______________________________

Claim the professor makes: ______________________________

____

Point 1: ______________________________

Example: ______________________________

____

Point 2: ______________________________

Example: ______________________________

____

prosperous:
rich; wealthy

civilization:
a society that has developed its own culture and achievements

flourish:
to grow or prosper

agriculture:
the practice of cultivating soil and raising crops

settle down:
to stay in a certain place

irrigation:
a water supply system

ditch:
a long narrow channel dug into the ground

forage:
to scavenge or look for food

import:
to bring or carry in from other lands

export:
to bring or send good to other lands

route:
a road or course

Step 2

Read and think about the prompt below. Answer the following questions in complete sentences.

Using points and examples from the lecture, describe how building near water sources benefited ancient cities.

1. What was the importance of water sources to ancient cities?

____

2. What is the reason that the Sumerian civilization formed?

____

3. According to the professor, how did water contribute to Egypt's success?

____

Step 3

Now create your own response to this topic using words and expressions from Steps 1 and 2.

The professor says ____.

First, ____. For example,

____. Because ____________________,

they ______________________________. Living close to ______________________________.

This ______________________________. The ______________, for example, ______________

______________________________. Therefore, ______________________________

____.

Now listen to a sample response. How does it differ from your response? Write down any differences in information or phrasing. Track 69

Notes

Listen again and repeat after the response. Pay close attention to pronunciation, intonation, and word stress. Track 70

Step 4

Now give your own spoken response to the prompt. Try to incorporate useful expressions from Step 3, while also paying attention to your pronunciation and intonation. Record your time.

Response: Speaking time: ______________ seconds

Vocabulary Review 3

Instructions: Choose the best word or phrase to complete each sentence.

1. The ______________ in front of the elementary school was undergoing renovations, so students had to stay inside during recess.

(A) campus
(B) playground
(C) lab
(D) museum

2. The president made a deal to ______________ fresh grapes into this country from California.

(A) import
(B) drain
(C) export
(D) concentrate

3. It was ______________ for the girl to write a 300-word essay in order for her to get accepted into the organization.

(A) prestigious
(B) accidental
(C) mandatory
(D) intentional

4. Even though the creatures in the movie were supposed to be ______________, I was not that scared.

(A) comical
(B) curious
(C) vulnerable
(D) fearsome

5. I prefer to go to the ______________ library because it only takes me fifteen minutes to walk there from my house.

(A) local
(B) typical
(C) minimal
(D) prestigious

6. Janet was listening to her CD player when it suddenly stopped. It was time to ______________ the battery.

(A) reclaim
(B) represent
(C) recharge
(D) release

7. Make sure that you ______________ hold the vase in your hand so you won't drop it.

(A) generally
(B) firmly
(C) specifically
(D) efficiently

8. King Arthur was a ______________ king of England who was known for his bravery and goodness.

(A) legendary
(B) fearsome
(C) competitive
(D) decorative

9. I was able to ______________ the entire alphabet from memory by the time I was four years old.

(A) memorize
(B) clarify
(C) theorize
(D) recite

10. The ______________ I gave him on how to improve his poster was to change his text to a bigger font.

(A) data
(B) suggestion
(C) component
(D) break

11. I'm not sure if I am ______________ to apply for a degree in literature, but I would like to apply if at all possible.

(A) eligible
(B) literary
(C) distinctive
(D) prosperous

12. Even though I did my best in high school, I was not able to ______________ the high grades that I wanted.

(A) encounter
(B) award
(C) attain
(D) dispute

13. In order to get my daily exercise, I ______________ all the way down the block to the store and back.

(A) forage
(B) jog
(C) facilitate
(D) flourish

14. Newspapers try to print the most ______________ news; otherwise, people begin to lose interest in subjects as more time elapses.

(A) noble
(B) timely
(C) various
(D) awkward

15. Sylvia recently graduated from State University. She managed to ______________ a bachelor's degree in liberal arts.

(A) acquire
(B) realize
(C) archive
(D) inquire

Instructions: Choose the word or phrase closest in meaning to the underlined word or phrase.

16. A turning door was put at the entrance of the hotel. It turns whenever anyone presses against it.

(A) expanding
(B) revolving
(C) twisting
(D) circling

17. Andrea was so busy that she didn't have time to proofread her paper before turning it in.

(A) uneasy
(B) exhausted
(C) overwhelming
(D) occupied

18. The psychologist advised her patients to practice self-esteem techniques each day before they went to school.

(A) security guard
(B) counselor
(C) judge
(D) neuroscientist

19. As the leader had so much work to do, he began to pass on many of the tasks to his workers.

(A) delegate
(B) post
(C) contend
(D) deter

20. The Middle East is often referred to as the Fertile Crescent. It's so known because it was the birthplace of the very first cities.

(A) agriculture
(B) irrigation
(C) cathedrals
(D) civilizations

21. Too much work is negative because people get so stressed out that they cannot perform adequate work.

(A) exasperating
(B) counterproductive
(C) anxious
(D) menacing

22. Whenever I baby-sit for young children, I always try to keep them entertained with various activities.

(A) charges
(B) toddlers
(C) applicants
(D) siblings

23. The noble gentlemen were common heroes in classical literature. They were usually the ones who were favored by the gods.

(A) aristocratic
(B) wealthy
(C) common
(D) heroic

24. I expect that I'll win at this game, since I've almost always won it in the past.

(A) theorize
(B) manipulate
(C) bet
(D) intervene

25. The substance of the report was disorganized, and there were many spelling errors.

(A) news
(B) task
(C) policy
(D) content

26. I was forced to choose between many diverse applicants. I couldn't make an appropriate decision.

(A) various
(B) separate
(C) similar
(D) opposite

27. The manager wanted to resolve the dispute between her workers in a professional way.

(A) degree
(B) issue
(C) trial
(D) manner

28. The recreational center had a new policy: anyone who wanted to sign up for an activity had to do so through the Internet.

(A) converse
(B) pursue
(C) enroll
(D) clarify

29. The mother tried to maintain a positive attitude, but she was finding it increasingly hard to do so.

(A) beverage
(B) lightness
(C) quality
(D) temper

30. Many of the students in my class don't apply themselves to their schoolwork.

(A) few
(B) some
(C) several
(D) select

Instructions: Write the missing words. Use the words below to fill in the blanks.

hard-wired	neuroscientists
permanent	tissue
adapt	cognitively
strokes	regenerate
cells	motor

The brain is truly a fascinating area of study, and **31.** _______________ are constantly astounded by the new discoveries they make. In fact, in the last few decades, they've discovered that adults can **32.** _______________ recover from brain damage. It used to be thought that brain damage was **33.** _______________ in adults. Adult brains are considered to be **34.** _______________ and are thus less likely to change. Yet now scientists know of at least two methods the adult brain can use to recover from brain damage. First, if a part of the brain is damaged, brain **35.** _______________ can **36.** _______________ to form new cells. These cells can help replace damaged brain **37.** _______________. Secondly, the brain is able to **38.** _______________ to compensate for damaged areas. This has been observed to occur frequently in people who have suffered from **39.** _______________. They have been able to recover certain **40.** _______________ skills that were once thought to be lost.

Instructions: Choose one word from each group that does not belong.

41. portray, depict, conceal, display

42. clarify, mystify, explain, illuminate

43. exasperating, infuriating, vexing, fulfilling

44. volleyball, soccer, tennis, swimming

45. comical, hilarious, sensible, ridiculous

Instructions: Label each pair of words as similar (S) or opposite (O).

46. __________ ditch mound

47. __________ excel surpass

48. __________ vulnerable invincible

49. __________ passion enthusiasm

50. __________ habit convention

Vocabulary Review 4

Instructions: Choose the best word or phrase to complete each sentence.

1. The ___________ was so bad that I couldn't see anything. I put on my hood to cover my face from the snow.

(A) tornado
(B) thunderstorm
(C) sandstorm
(D) blizzard

2. Strict dominance hierarchies can perhaps best be observed in the ___________ species. These large primates live in both the savanna and in the jungle.

(A) monkey
(B) baboon
(C) chimpanzee
(E) human

3. The ___________ news that I just heard today is that the stock market is experiencing an all-time low.

(A) current
(B) timely
(C) inconvenient
(D) instant

4. According to one theory, people need to be able to display ___________ in order to be effective leaders.

(A) visions
(B) dominance
(C) charisma
(D) imagination

5. The beautiful mountains completely ___________ me, so that I completely forgot where I was and what I was doing.

(A) unnerved
(B) captivated
(C) concerned
(D) grabbed

6. As I got an A on my mid-term, I was able to raise my class grade to an A-. This will significantly increase my ___________.

(A) extra credit grade
(B) transcript
(C) scholarship
(D) GPA

7. For the moment, I am content with my job as an assistant manager. ___________, however, I would like to go on to manage my own company.

(A) rapidly
(B) precisely
(C) eventually
(D) immediately

8. His logic was so sound that nobody dared to ___________ him because they were afraid of getting humiliated.

(A) argue
(B) dispute
(C) assent
(D) cooperate

9. In wartime, ___________ can be an efficient vehicle to use because of their sturdiness and their ability to get people to places quickly.

(A) a jeep
(B) a motorcycle
(C) a bus
(D) a train

10. James knew that it would be hard work, but he was determined to get his ___________ degree. It was the highest degree that he could earn.

(A) doctoral
(B) associate
(C) bachelor's
(D) master's

11. I'm not certain what type of characteristics the color green ____________, but I associate the color with life and re-growth.

(A) means
(B) defines
(C) embodies
(D) informs

12. Glen often lost his temper and got himself in trouble. For this reason, he worked extra hard to handle his disputes more ____________.

(A) rationally
(B) generally
(C) efficiently
(D) drastically

13. The new company was sending a ____________ of machine components overseas to its first foreign client.

(A) payload
(B) cargo
(C) weight
(D) luggage

14. One product that has become quite popular in big buildings or warehouses is ____________ lamps. These skinny lamps give off light more efficiently than other types of lamps.

(A) fluorescent
(B) antique
(C) modern
(D) ultraviolet

15. Nearly all communal animals have some sort of ____________. These are needed to maintain order within the group.

(A) society
(B) government
(C) social structure
(D) territory

Instructions: Choose the word closest in meaning to the underlined word or phrase.

16. No one was really sure how the scientist had <u>come up with</u> his theory, but it seemed to work in every tested experiment.

(A) conspired
(B) diagrammed
(C) plotted
(D) devised

17. I think it would be more <u>financially beneficial</u> to wait to invest in the stock until after it has gone down in price.

(A) advantageous
(B) profitable
(C) available
(D) positive

18. My sister's favorite thing to do when we go to the beach is to <u>float</u> in the water and let the waves push her back and forth.

(A) drift
(B) sink
(C) flow
(D) cruise

19. The <u>gathering of people</u> was so large that Amelia couldn't see the stage. She had to stand up on a chair in order to see anything.

(A) heap
(B) crowd
(C) collection
(D) size

20. The <u>buildup</u> of rust on the nail caused it to break. As a result, the picture fell off the wall.

(A) distribution
(B) deposit
(C) hoard
(D) display

21. Shelley agreed with her manager's opinion: it was time to expand the company.

(A) concurred
(B) permitted
(C) refuted
(D) corresponded

22. The man's signature was so unique that nobody could even come close to copying it.

(A) characteristic
(B) peculiar
(C) surprising
(D) distinctive

23. The man's cousin angers him so much that he hardly ever likes to go to family gatherings.

(A) ancestor
(B) relative
(C) spouse
(D) successor

24. The hot liquid mass of lava burst forth from the volcano and destroyed the abandoned town.

(A) bubbling
(B) festering
(C) molten
(D) seething

25. Emily walked back to her room at the college to put her school things away, and then she hurried to her next appointment.

(A) dorm
(B) lobby
(C) office
(D) lab

26. The Earth is made up of many plates. When these plates slip past each other, even if it's only slightly, it can cause earthquakes.

(A) fall
(B) bend
(C) sneak
(D) shift

27. George has a propensity for leaving his clothes out around the house, even though his mother continually reminds him to put them away.

(A) preference
(B) custom
(C) convention
(D) tendency

28. My mother witnessed personally the launch of the space shuttle to the moon in 1969.

(A) individually
(B) specifically
(C) firsthand
(D) obviously

29. Once the Greeks came into power, they established an elaborate system of trade between the different countries of the Mediterranean.

(A) network
(B) association
(C) organization
(D) approach

30. Although Judith hoped that college would help her to get a good job, she mainly wanted to go to better herself as a person.

(A) effectively
(B) roughly
(C) broadly
(D) primarily

Instructions: Write the missing words. Use the words below to fill in the blanks.

encounter	facilitate
campus	assistance
impact	escort
park	applicants
pool	transition

Adjusting to college can significantly **31.** ______________ the lives of ncoming freshmen. Therefore, it may be helpful for these students to seek **32.** ______________ from people who have already graduated from college, like parents or friends. These people could **33.** ______________ the **34.** ______________ from high school to college. Probably the first advice they would give to high school students who are applying to college is to create a creative admissions essay. **35.** ______________ who are creative make their essays stand out from a **36.** ______________ of other admissions essays. Next, students may find it helpful to purchase a parking pass so they can **37.** ______________ on **38.** ______________. Also, parents and friends will probably point out that students often **39.** ______________ lots of stress in college, so students need to be sure to ask for plenty of help and support from loved ones if they feel overwhelmed. Also, students should remember never to compromise their safety. In fact, it is beneficial for students who take night classes to request a(n) **40.** ______________ to walk them back to their cars.

Instructions: Use the words below to fill in the blanks.

back	out	up	down	off

41. Phil was hoping to hang ____________ with Barbara once class was over.

42. Mark showed ____________ his talent as a magician by performing magic tricks in class.

43. Whenever I go to the gas station, I always fill ____________ my gas tank with premium gasoline.

44. The teacher asked the unruly children to please settle ____________ or else face punishment.

45. The fossil dated ____________ all the way to twelve million years ago.

Instructions: Match the words that have opposite meanings.

46. sympathetic	(A) avoid
47. prominent	(B) humble
48. aristocratic	(C) premature
49. access	(D) anonymous
50. overdue	(E) insensitive

Part 3
Speaking Naturally

Chapter 7	Pronunciation
Chapter 8	Stress and Intonation
Chapter 9	Pausing

The tips below can help you to improve both your fluency and clarity of speech:

During the speech:

- Open your mouth while speaking. Try not to mumble.
- Pay special attention to the pronunciation of content words and key terms.
- Stress each syllable correctly and accurately.
- Clearly pronounce both vowels and consonants.
- Smoothly link sounds between words within a phrase and in consonant clusters.
- Change pitch between stressed and unstressed syllables.
- Speak in sentences or phrases, not word by word.
- Speak with appropriate speed, not too quickly.

When practicing:

- Practice speaking by writing down every word you say and marking each place where you pause or vary intonation.
- Examine this transcript of your speech and look for possible mistakes. Practice these parts again, focusing on correcting the previous mistakes.
- Record and listen to your speech. Note any areas for improvement.

Stress and intonation are very important in English. The rhythm of sentences spoken in English alerts listeners to the message presented. Words or phrases important to the content of the message tend to be stressed, whereas words or phrases that are not important tend to be reduced.

Chapter 7 Pronunciation

Stress on content words

Certain words within a sentence are given importance because of the meaning they communicate. These words are referred to as content words. Words with little or no meaning outside their grammatical function are usually not stressed within the sentence.

→ **Content words:** nouns, verbs, adjectives, adverbs

→ **Function words:** modal auxiliary verbs, "be" verbs, most pronouns, prepositions, articles

Stressed syllables are pronounced longer, pitched higher, and spoken slightly louder.

▸ Step 1

Listen to the sentences and underline the words that are stressed. Track 71

1. However, I would definitely like to go to the park on my new scooter.
2. After this annual seminar is over, please do not forget to sign up for the one next year.
3. The small child was uncertain as to whether or not he should raise his hand.
4. I think it is better to keep a calendar in order to remember important dates.
5. My grandparents significantly influenced my happiness as a child.
6. Although I would like to take Saturday off, I believe it is more important that I go to the tutoring session.
7. So far, my experiences with skydiving have been fun and exciting.
8. The professor must conduct lots of research in order to publish his findings.

Listen again and repeat the sentences.

▸ Step 2

Listen to the paragraph. Write only the words you hear most clearly. Track 72

____

____

____

____

Stress on function words

> The normal pattern of sentence stress reduces function words. However, function words can be stressed when the speaker is expressing strong emotion, is disagreeing, or is clarifying mistaken information.
>
> **Ex.** Don't you agree that English is easy?
>
> I do not agree! (Non-contracted forms are often used to show stress).

Step 1

Listen to the following sentences and indicate whether each underlined word is reduced (R) or stressed (S). Track 73

1. However, Roger should know how to wash his own clothes. ______
2. Actually, I did guess many of the correct answers on yesterday's test. ______
3. Fifty years ago, my grandparents were married in Hawaii. ______
4. I am ready to register for my classes next week. ______
5. Despite evidence to the contrary, George is certain that he will get picked for the part. ______
6. He is not the one with the cold. I am. ______
7. I could participate in the game, but I really don't want to play. ______ ______
8. Should you decide to attend the seminar, you will need to present a report. ______

Listen again and repeat the sentences.

Step 2

Listen to the following sentences. Circle any underlined words that should be stressed. More than one word may be stressed in each sentence. Track 74

Example: Even though he did not win the marathon, he (did) win a trophy for second place.

1. I know you think I cannot do it, but I really can handle an after-school job.
2. Last year, it both rained and snowed during the month of June.
3. Are you absolutely certain that you cannot make the meeting today?
4. She prefers cleaning her bedroom over cleaning her bathroom.
5. I have so much homework that I do not know where to start.
6. It is impossible to trust anything that my best friend says.
7. Marketing 413 is only for business majors.
8. The instructor taught the girl to play the piano beautifully.

Listen again and repeat the sentences.

Intonation is also very important to English. The pitch of the speaker's voice alerts listeners to the particular message being conveyed. By modifying the pitch of the voice to rise, fall, or do both, the speaker stresses certain words and meanings. When modifying the pitch, the speaker often lengthens the amount of time each word is pronounced.

Chapter 8 Stress and Intonation

Changing pitch for emphasis

At the beginning of a conversation, the last content word in each sentence is usually the focus of meaning. Therefore, the primary stress in these sentences usually falls on the last content word. The sound of the speaker's voice rises on the focus word and then falls. If the sentence is a question, the sound of the speaker's voice rises but does not fall at the end of the sentence.

Ex. Is that a <u>deer</u>? No, it is a big <u>dog</u>.

However, the focus of a sentence can change. Thus, one sentence can have more than one intonation pattern. By noticing the word the speaker emphasizes, the listener can guess what will come next.

Ex. It is not <u>small</u> dog. It is a <u>big</u> dog.

▶ Step 1

Listen to the first sentence and underline the focus word. Then choose the sentence most likely to come next. Track 75

1. It is a bad idea to wait until the night before a test to begin studying.
a. Tests are some of the hardest parts of school.
b. It is also not wise to wait until the last minute to do homework.

2. Teenagers should have certain restrictions on their driver's licenses.
a. Children should not be allowed to smoke until they reach adulthood.
b. However, those over 18 do not need any driving restrictions.

3. Are you sure you do not want to have lunch with me?
a. No, lunch is not until one o'clock.
b. No, I am eating lunch with another friend.

4. That is a really large piece of cake.
a. Actually, I made the cake for somebody else.
b. It is way too much for me to eat.

Listen again and repeat the sentences. Ensure your voice is rising on the stressed syllables and dropping afterwards.

▸ Step 2

Read the two sentences. Try to figure out how the second sentence relates to the first. Underline the focus word in the first sentence according to this context.

1. The recreational center will offer a new self-defense course. It will teach young people how to protect themselves.
2. Butterflies are usually active during the day. Moths are more active at night.
3. I prefer not to have homework over the weekends. However, I do not mind having a little bit of homework then.
4. Everyone wants to buy a beautiful house. For this reason, houses that are ugly do not sell very well.
5. The fifth-grader was a very messy worker. Her partner was very organized.
6. The woman bought a new bag at the mall downtown. It had just opened a couple of weeks before.

Listen and repeat the sentences. Ensure your voice is rising on the stressed syllables and dropping afterwards. Track 76

Commas and series with *and* or *or*

When there is a series of words with the conjunctions *and* or *or*, the intonation rises on all members of the series except the last. The last member has a rising-falling intonation.

Ex. We went to the park, / (↗) the beach, / (↗) and the mountains. (↘)
You can do it Monday / (↗) or Tuesday. (↘)

After the comma used between a sentence and an additional phrase, the intonation rises.

Ex. It is three blocks from here, / (↗) near the supermarket. (↘)
As for me, / (↗) I will have the soup and salad. (↘).

▶ Step 1

Divide the sentences into thought groups by using slashes (/) and mark the intonation of each group with arrows (↗ or ↘).

1. The man's chores included walking the dog, doing the laundry, cleaning the bathroom, and washing the car.
2. Recycling campaigns have been very successful in our city, partially due to the friendly publicity from local newspapers.
3. I was not certain whether the text should be placed at the top of the page or in the middle.
4. Young people often experience pressure from outside influences to conform to certain trends, particularly when they get into high school.
5. He could have told his mother that he had spent the evening studying, but it would not have been the truth.
6. The man was not sure whether to pick the striped tie, the green tie, or the purple tie.

Listen and repeat the sentences. Track 77

Having appropriate pauses is also an important part of spoken English. Pauses are given after each message unit in order to give listeners time to process the information. If a speaker speaks too rapidly or without thought to the grouping of the information presented, listeners may have difficulty distinguishing the important content of the message.

Chapter 9 Pausing

Pausing, like stress and pronunciation, greatly adds to the clarity of speech. There are several reasons for adding a pause:

→ To make the meaning clear: **Ex.** When the wind blows *[pause]* the waves run high.

→ For emphasis: **Ex.** Frankly *[pause]* I am disappointed in you.

→ To enable the speaker to catch a breath

→ To give listeners time to understand complex sentences

Therefore, it is helpful to pause after commas, transitional words, and complicated ideas, such as lengthy subjects, prepositional phrases, and clauses in compound and complex sentences.

Step 1

Look at the following sentences and circle any (/) that indicates an appropriate pause.

1. Although the Greeks / were credited with the first Western democracy / neither women / nor slaves had the right / to vote.
2. During the debate / the woman proved that Jason's argument was flawed / thereby embarrassing him / in front of everyone.
3. Those pineapples were / in my opinion / the best fruit / that I had ever tasted.
4. Many critics believe / that modern movies lack / what early movies possessed / namely / a strong plot and good actors.
5. Common pets / in American households include birds / cats / and dogs.
6. Nevertheless / I still do not agree that animal testing / is worthwhile.

Listen and repeat the sentences. Track 78

▶ Step 2

Practice saying the sample response and write a slash (/) where you would pause.

1. His ability to track creatures across long distances enabled the man to compete in an annual competition where contestants tracked certain animals.
2. Many scientists contend that the universe started with a big bang, releasing enormous amounts of energy to create the solar systems and planets.
3. In the last three years, Joe's friends not only supported him during his illness, but they did everything in their power to make life easier for him so that he could recover more quickly.
4. Neela, a foreign exchange student from India, came from a small village in the mountains that depended almost entirely on farming.

Listen and repeat the sentences. Track 79

Pause and pitch

Every clause or thought group within a sentence contains a focus word. A rise and then a fall in pitch is used to mark this focus word. This change alerts listeners to the central meaning of the thought group. The fall in intonation, combined with pausing, helps listeners recognize the end of a thought group.

Ex. I remembered to bring paper, / but I forgot my book.
When the water boils rapidly, / put the spaghetti in the pot.
When the water boils, / rapidly put the spaghetti in the pot.

Step 1

Practice saying the sentences. Be sure to use appropriate pauses and pitch.

1. Remember that when the timer rings, it is time to give the baby his bottle.
2. Ultimately, a person's success in life depends on two things: hard work and dedication.
3. Albert Einstein, the scientist known for his strange hair, came up with his theory of relativity in 1915.
4. A college education should be provided for by the government, according to my economics teacher, Ms. Brown.
5. Since she had disobeyed her parents earlier, Emily was forbidden to leave her room for the rest of the night.
6. On the other hand, I do not believe that art should replace reading, writing, and arithmetic as a student's main priorities in school.

Listen and repeat the sentences. Track 80

Mastering Skills for the TOEFL® iBT

SPEAKING

Practice Tests

Practice Test 1

Track 81

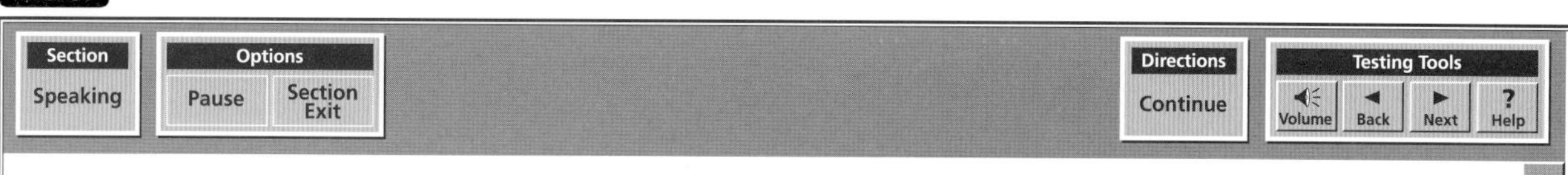

Speaking Section

Directions

In this section of the test, you will demonstrate your ability to speak about a variety of topics. You will answer six questions by speaking into the microphone. Answer each question as completely as possible.

In questions one and two, you will speak about familiar topics. Your response will be scored on your ability to speak clearly and coherently about the topics.

In questions three and four, you will first read a short text. The text will disappear, and you will then listen to a talk on the same topic. You will be asked a question about what you have read and heard. You will need to combine appropriate information from the text and the talk to provide a complete answer to the question. Your response is scored on your ability to speak clearly and coherently and on your ability to accurately convey information about what you read and heard.

In questions five and six, you will listen to part of a conversation or a lecture. You will be asked a question about what you heard. Your response is scored on your ability to speak clearly and coherently and on your ability to accurately convey information about what you heard.

You may take notes while you read and while you listen to the conversations and lectures. You may use your notes to help prepare your responses.

Listen carefully to the directions for each question. The directions are not shown on the screen.

For each question, you will be given a short time to prepare your response. A clock will show how much preparation time is remaining. When the preparation time is up, you will be told to begin your response. A clock will show how much time is remaining. A message will appear on the screen when the response time has ended.

If you finish before the allotted time, press **Continue** to go to the next question.

Question 1 Track 82

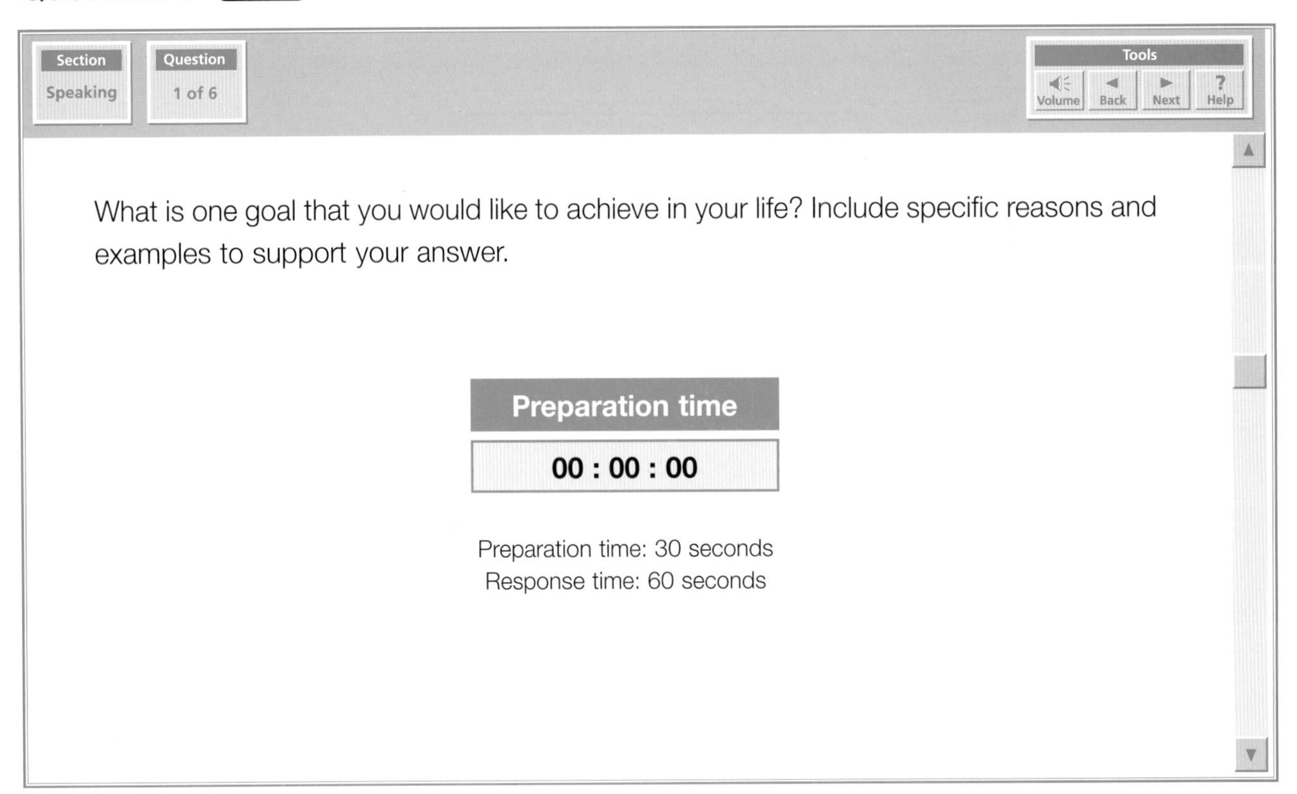

Question 2 Track 83

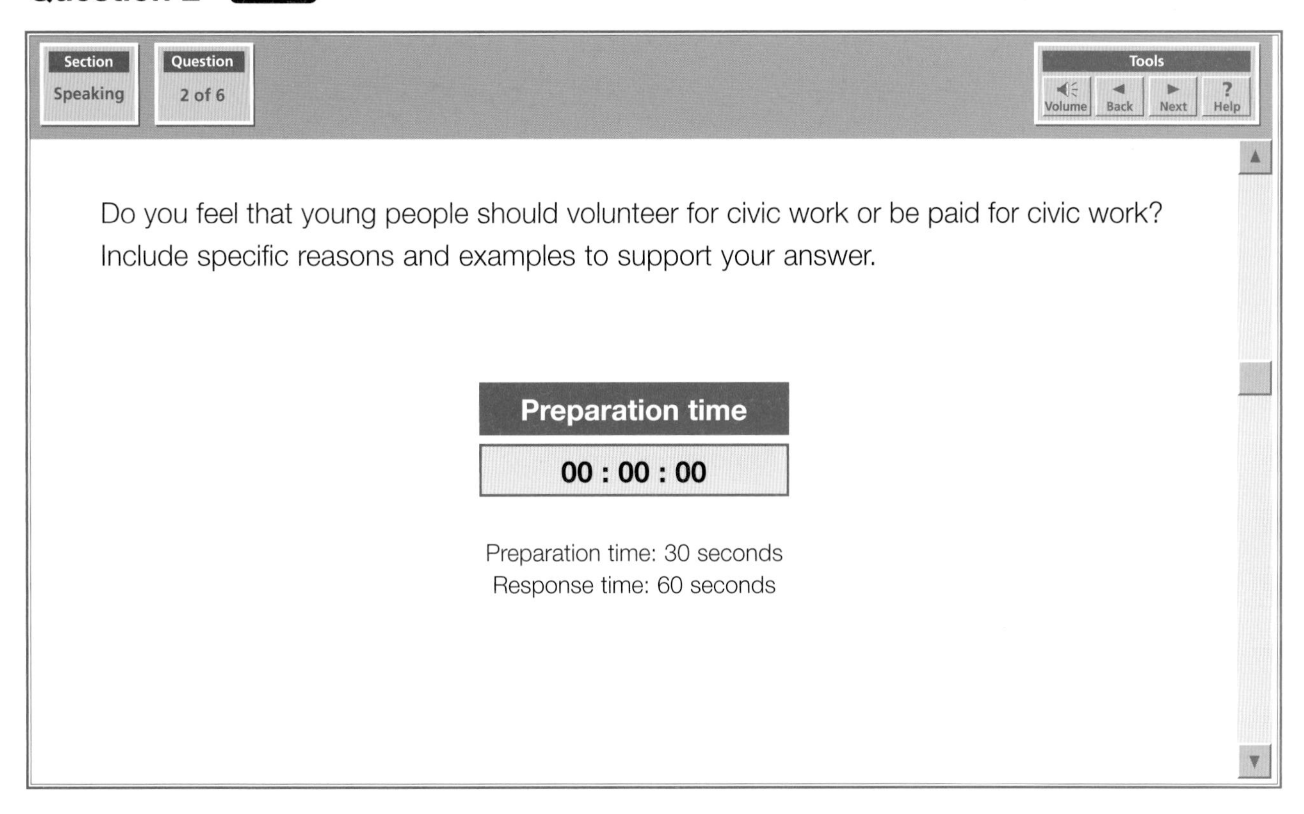

Question 3 Track 84

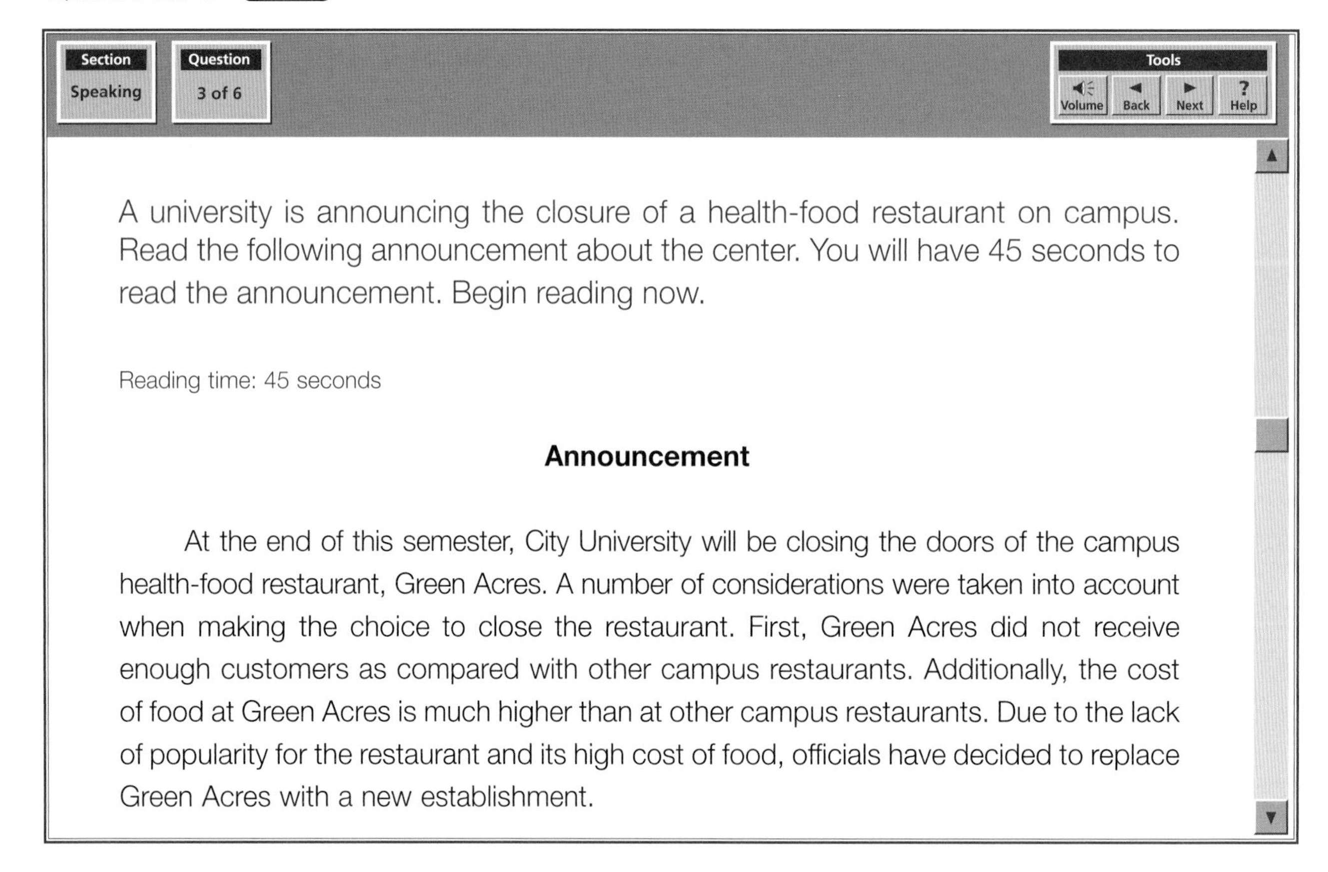
Section
Speaking
Question
3 of 6
Tools
Volume Back Next Help

A university is announcing the closure of a health-food restaurant on campus. Read the following announcement about the center. You will have 45 seconds to read the announcement. Begin reading now.

Reading time: 45 seconds

Announcement

At the end of this semester, City University will be closing the doors of the campus health-food restaurant, Green Acres. A number of considerations were taken into account when making the choice to close the restaurant. First, Green Acres did not receive enough customers as compared with other campus restaurants. Additionally, the cost of food at Green Acres is much higher than at other campus restaurants. Due to the lack of popularity for the restaurant and its high cost of food, officials have decided to replace Green Acres with a new establishment.

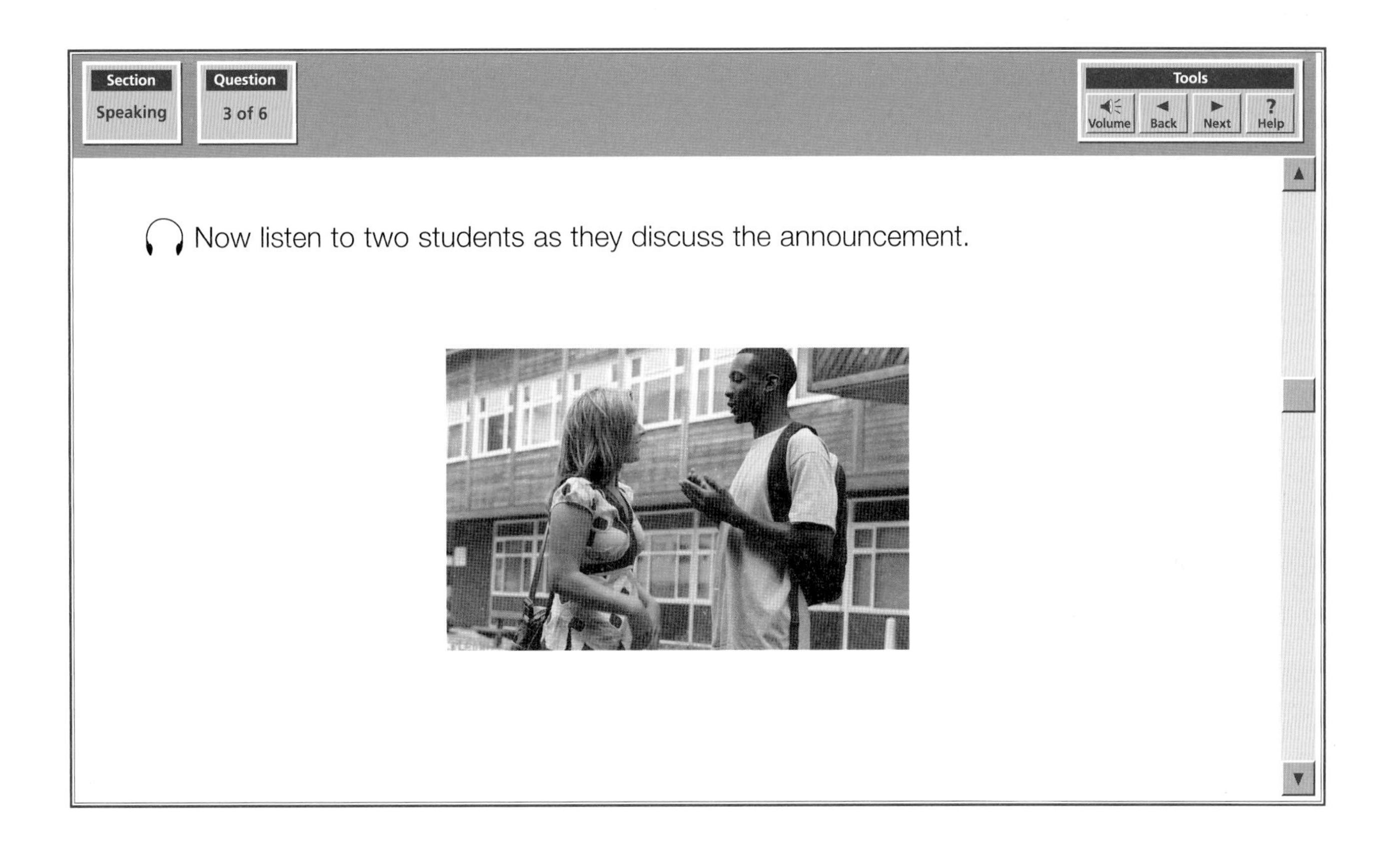
Section
Speaking
Question
3 of 6
Tools
Volume
Back
Next
Help
Now listen to two students as they discuss the announcement.

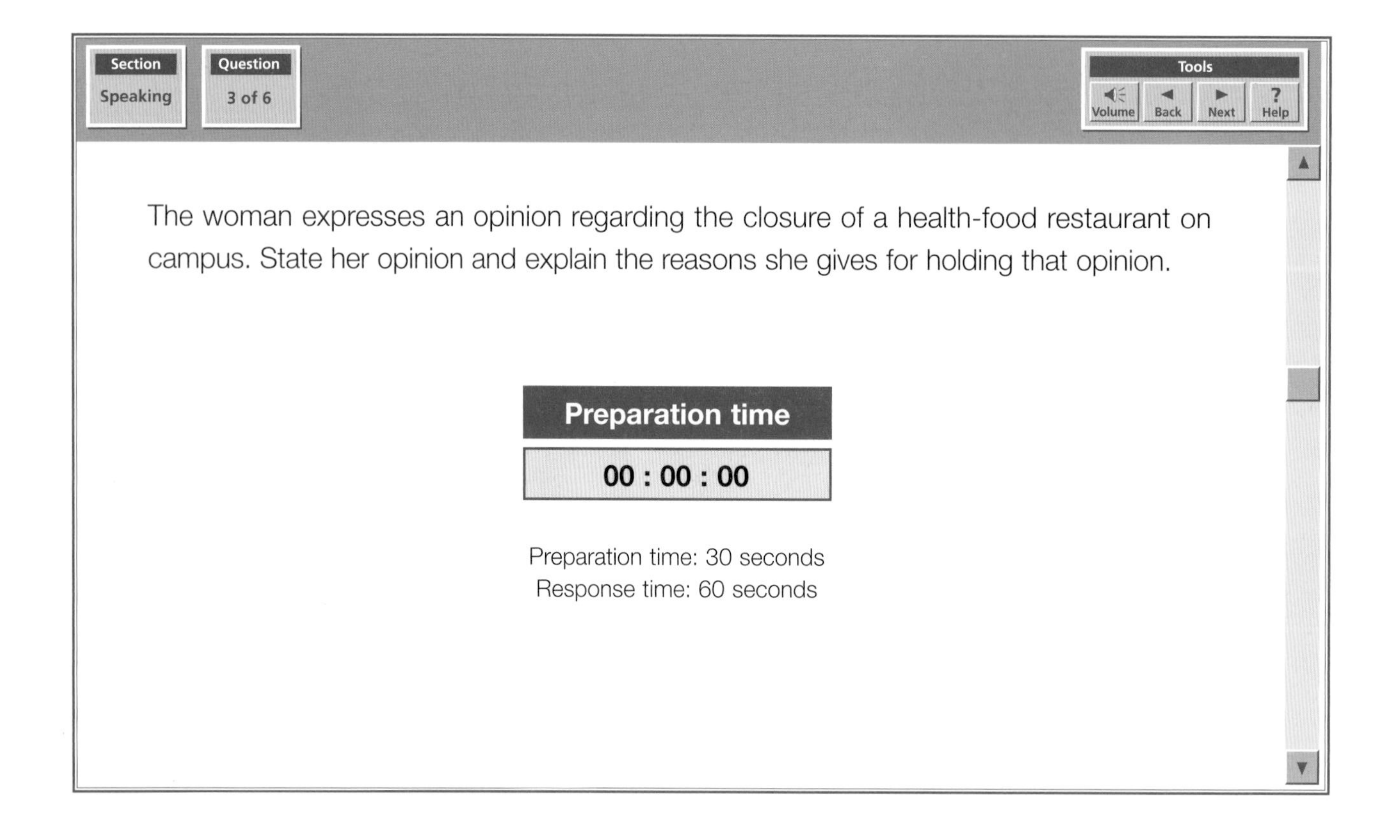
Section
Speaking
Question
3 of 6
Tools
Volume
Back
Next
Help
The woman expresses an opinion regarding the closure of a health-food restaurant on campus. State her opinion and explain the reasons she gives for holding that opinion.
Preparation time
00 : 00 : 00
Preparation time: 30 seconds
Response time: 60 seconds

Question 4 Track 85

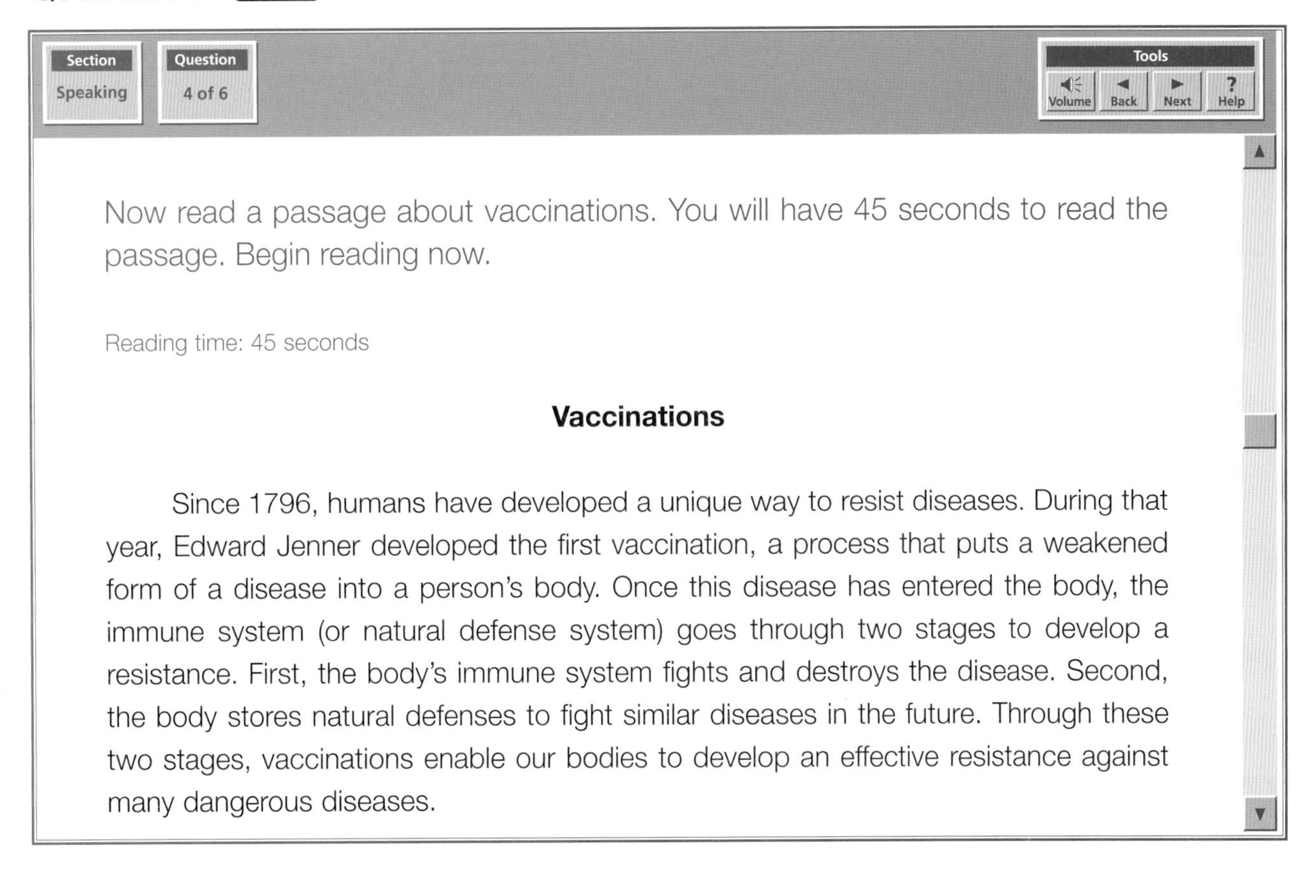

Now read a passage about vaccinations. You will have 45 seconds to read the passage. Begin reading now.

Reading time: 45 seconds

Vaccinations

Since 1796, humans have developed a unique way to resist diseases. During that year, Edward Jenner developed the first vaccination, a process that puts a weakened form of a disease into a person's body. Once this disease has entered the body, the immune system (or natural defense system) goes through two stages to develop a resistance. First, the body's immune system fights and destroys the disease. Second, the body stores natural defenses to fight similar diseases in the future. Through these two stages, vaccinations enable our bodies to develop an effective resistance against many dangerous diseases.

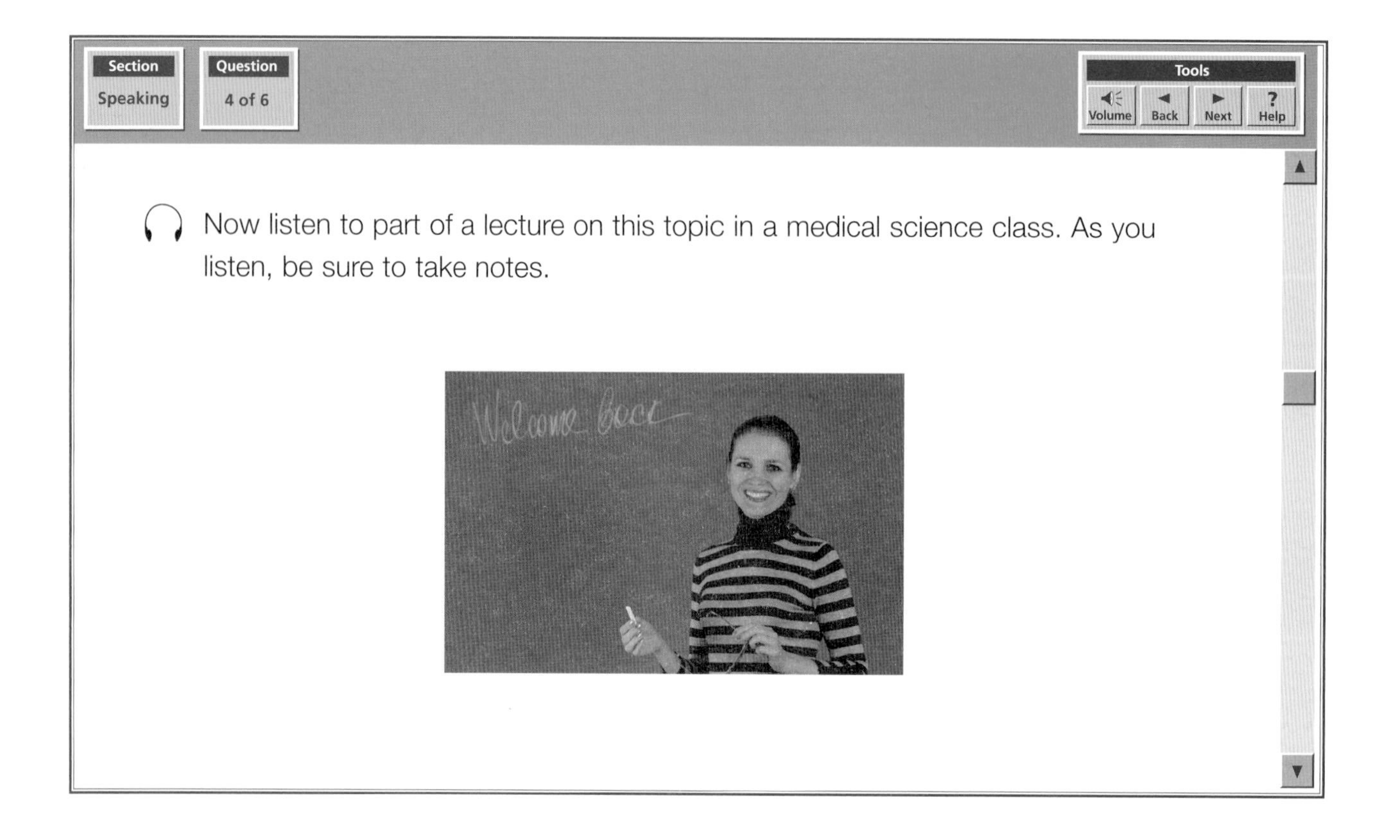
Section
Speaking
Question
4 of 6
Tools
Volume
Back
Next
Help
Now listen to part of a lecture on this topic in a medical science class. As you listen, be sure to take notes.

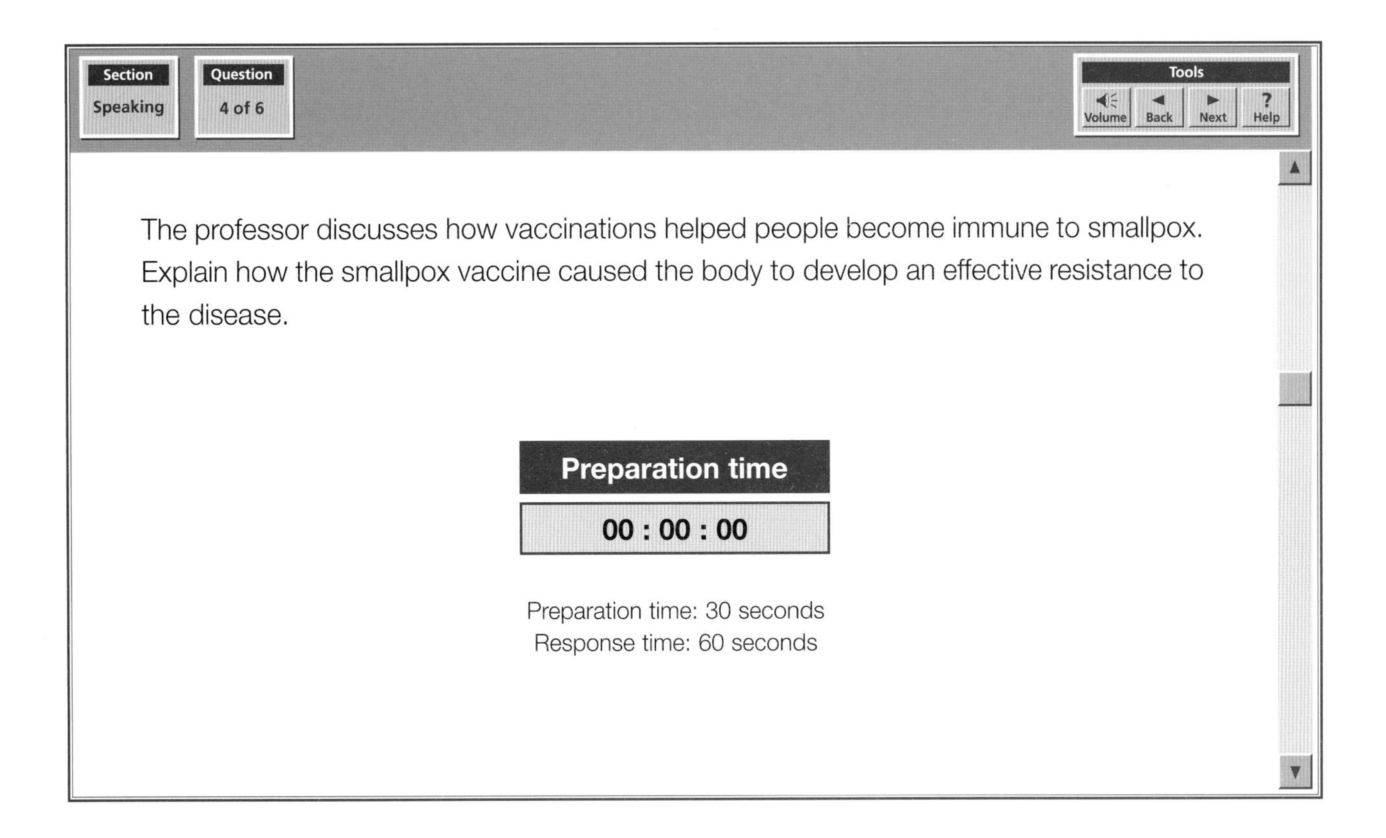
Section
Speaking
Question
4 of 6
Tools
Volume
Back
Next
Help
The professor discusses how vaccinations helped people become immune to smallpox. Explain how the smallpox vaccine caused the body to develop an effective resistance to the disease.
Preparation time
00 : 00 : 00
Preparation time: 30 seconds
Response time: 60 seconds

Question 5 Track 86

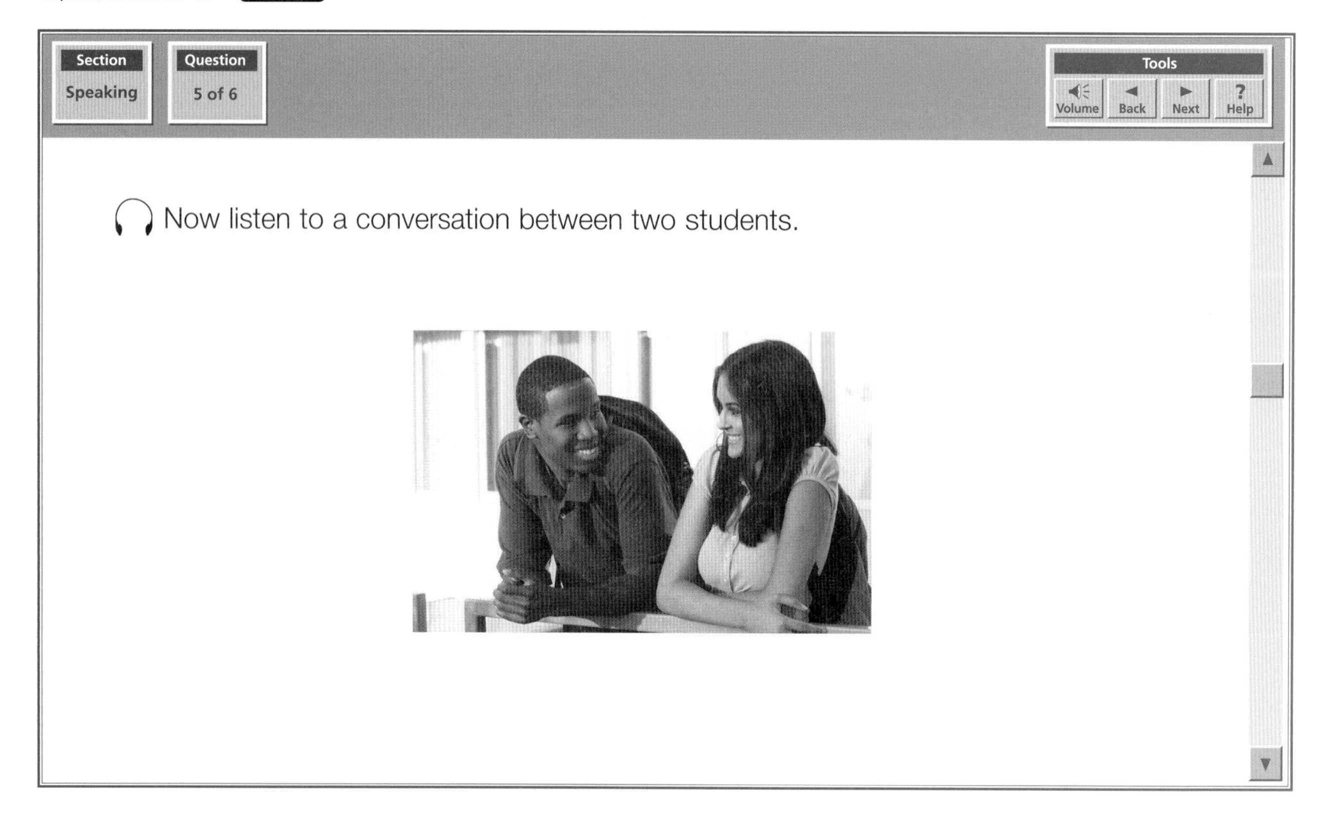

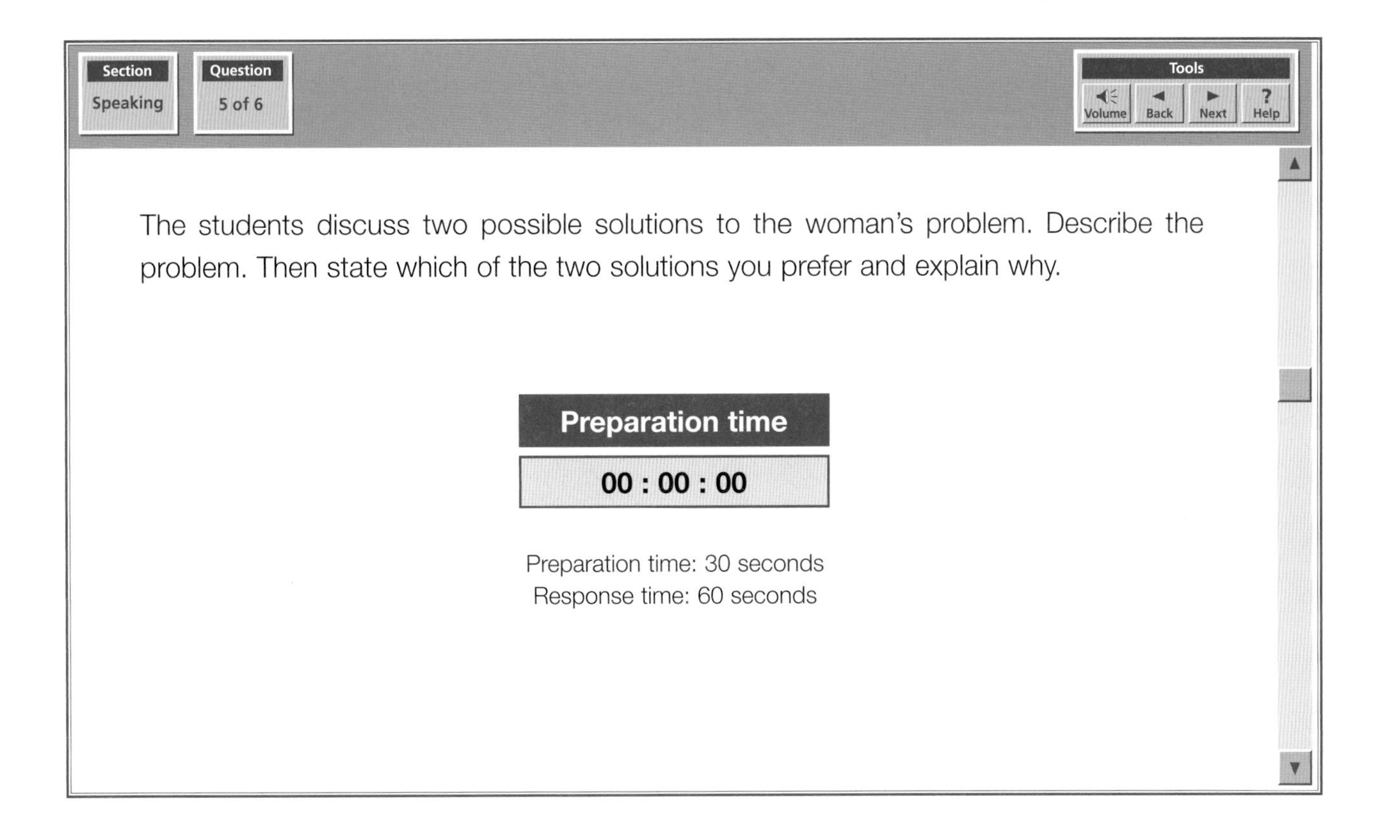
Section
Speaking
Question
5 of 6
Tools
Volume
Back
Next
Help
The students discuss two possible solutions to the woman's problem. Describe the problem. Then state which of the two solutions you prefer and explain why.
Preparation time
00 : 00 : 00
Preparation time: 30 seconds
Response time: 60 seconds

Question 6 Track 87

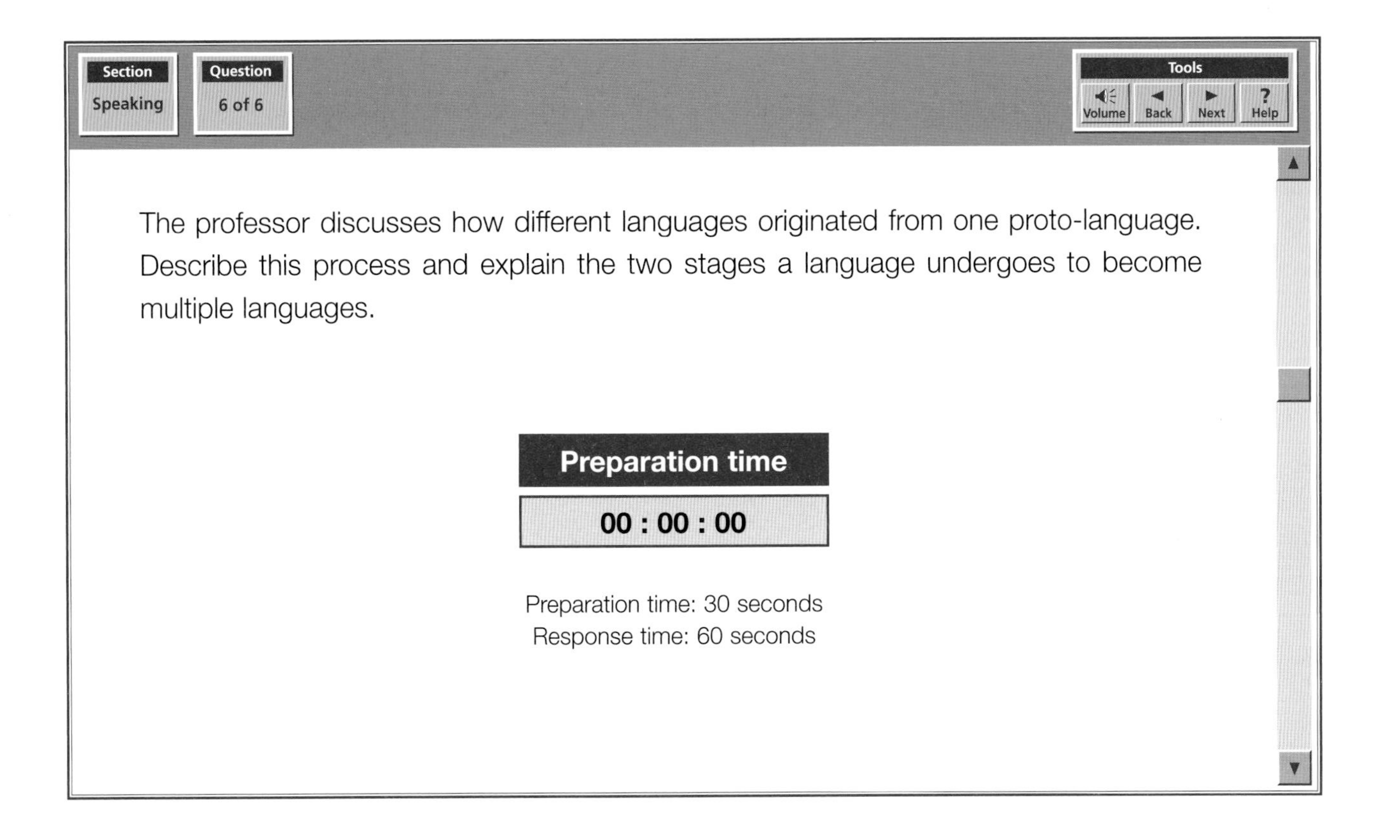
Section
Speaking
Question
6 of 6
Tools
Volume
Back
Next
Help
The professor discusses how different languages originated from one proto-language. Describe this process and explain the two stages a language undergoes to become multiple languages.
Preparation time
00 : 00 : 00
Preparation time: 30 seconds
Response time: 60 seconds

Practice Test 2

Track 88

Section: Speaking | Options: Pause, Section Exit | Directions: Continue | Testing Tools: Volume, Back, Next, Help

Speaking Section

Directions

In this section of the test, you will demonstrate your ability to speak about a variety of topics. You will answer six questions by speaking into the microphone. Answer each question as completely as possible.

In questions one and two, you will speak about familiar topics. Your response will be scored on your ability to speak clearly and coherently about the topics.

In questions three and four, you will first read a short text. The text will disappear, and you will then listen to a talk on the same topic. You will be asked a question about what you have read and heard. You will need to combine appropriate information from the text and the talk to provide a complete answer to the question. Your response is scored on your ability to speak clearly and coherently and on your ability to accurately convey information about what you read and heard.

In questions five and six, you will listen to part of a conversation or a lecture. You will be asked a question about what you heard. Your response is scored on your ability to speak clearly and coherently and on your ability to accurately convey information about what you heard.

You may take notes while you read and while you listen to the conversations and lectures. You may use your notes to help prepare your responses.

Listen carefully to the directions for each question. The directions are not shown on the screen.

For each question, you will be given a short time to prepare your response. A clock will show how much preparation time is remaining. When the preparation time is up, you will be told to begin your response. A clock will show how much time is remaining. A message will appear on the screen when the response time has ended.

If you finish before the allotted time, press **Continue** to go to the next question.

Question 1 Track 89

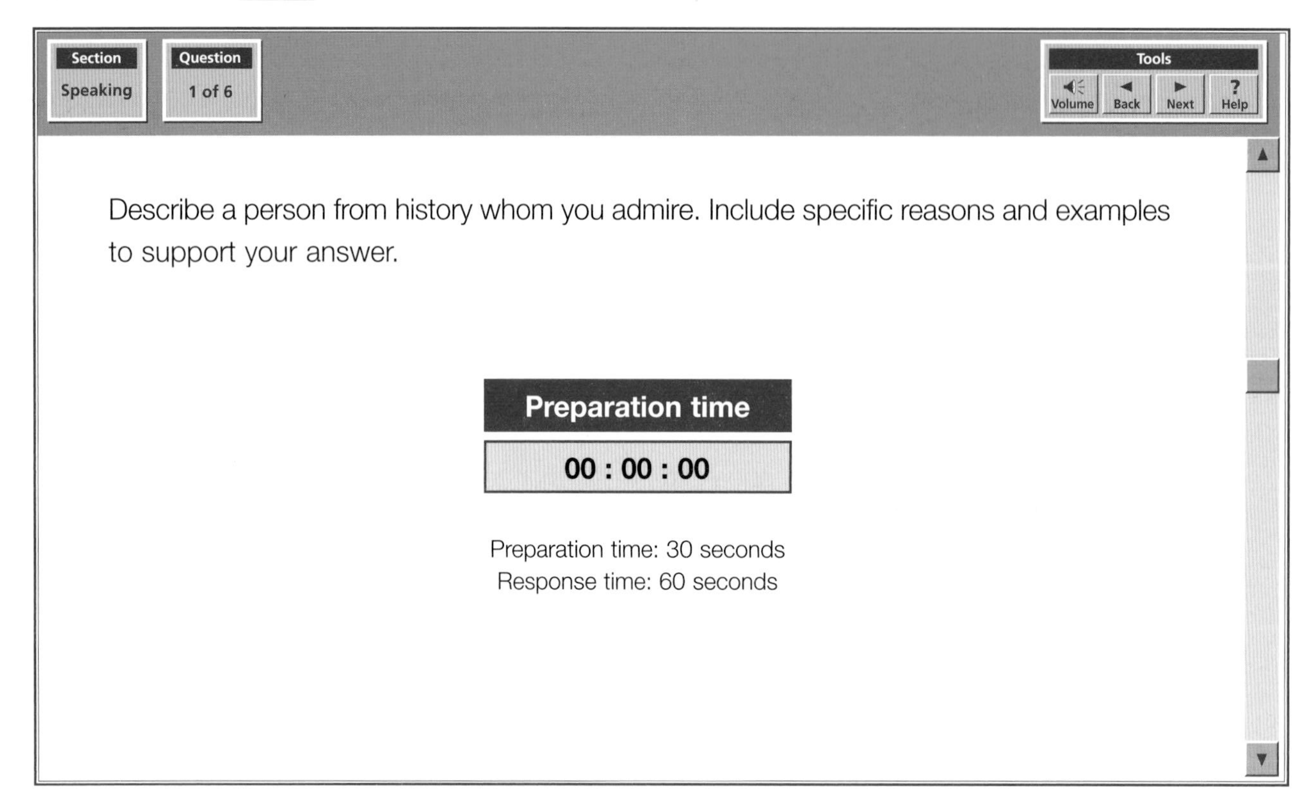

Question 2 Track 90

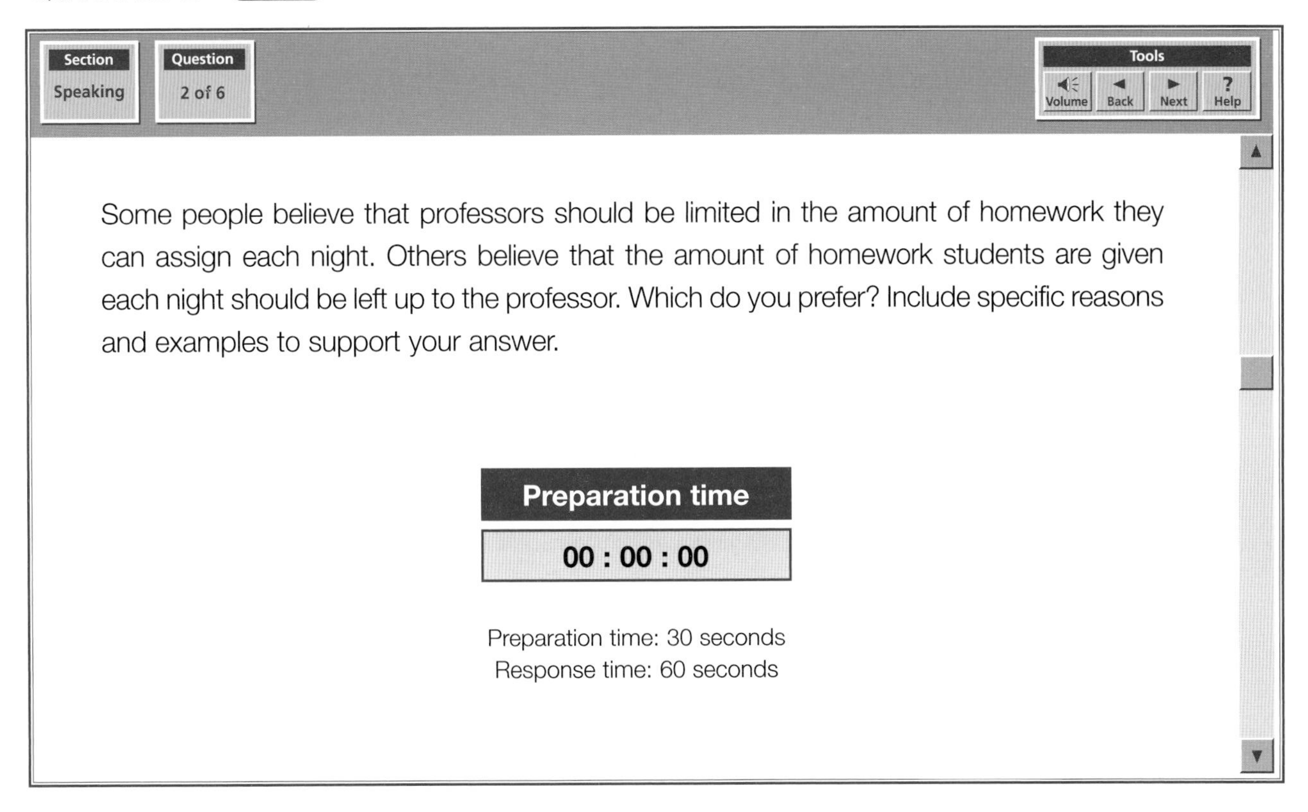

Question 3 Track 91

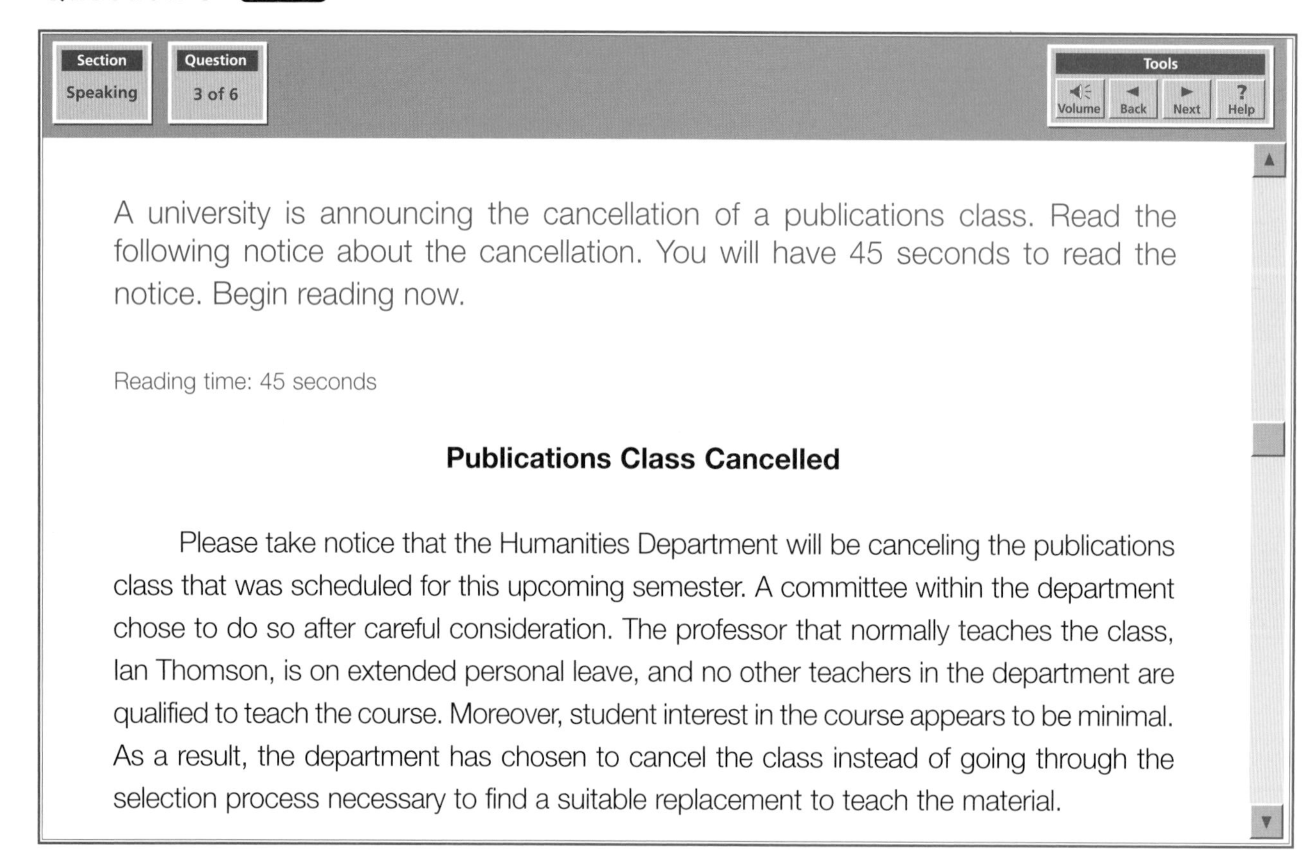
Section
Speaking
Question
3 of 6
Tools
Volume
Back
Next
Help

A university is announcing the cancellation of a publications class. Read the following notice about the cancellation. You will have 45 seconds to read the notice. Begin reading now.

Reading time: 45 seconds

Publications Class Cancelled

Please take notice that the Humanities Department will be canceling the publications class that was scheduled for this upcoming semester. A committee within the department chose to do so after careful consideration. The professor that normally teaches the class, Ian Thomson, is on extended personal leave, and no other teachers in the department are qualified to teach the course. Moreover, student interest in the course appears to be minimal. As a result, the department has chosen to cancel the class instead of going through the selection process necessary to find a suitable replacement to teach the material.

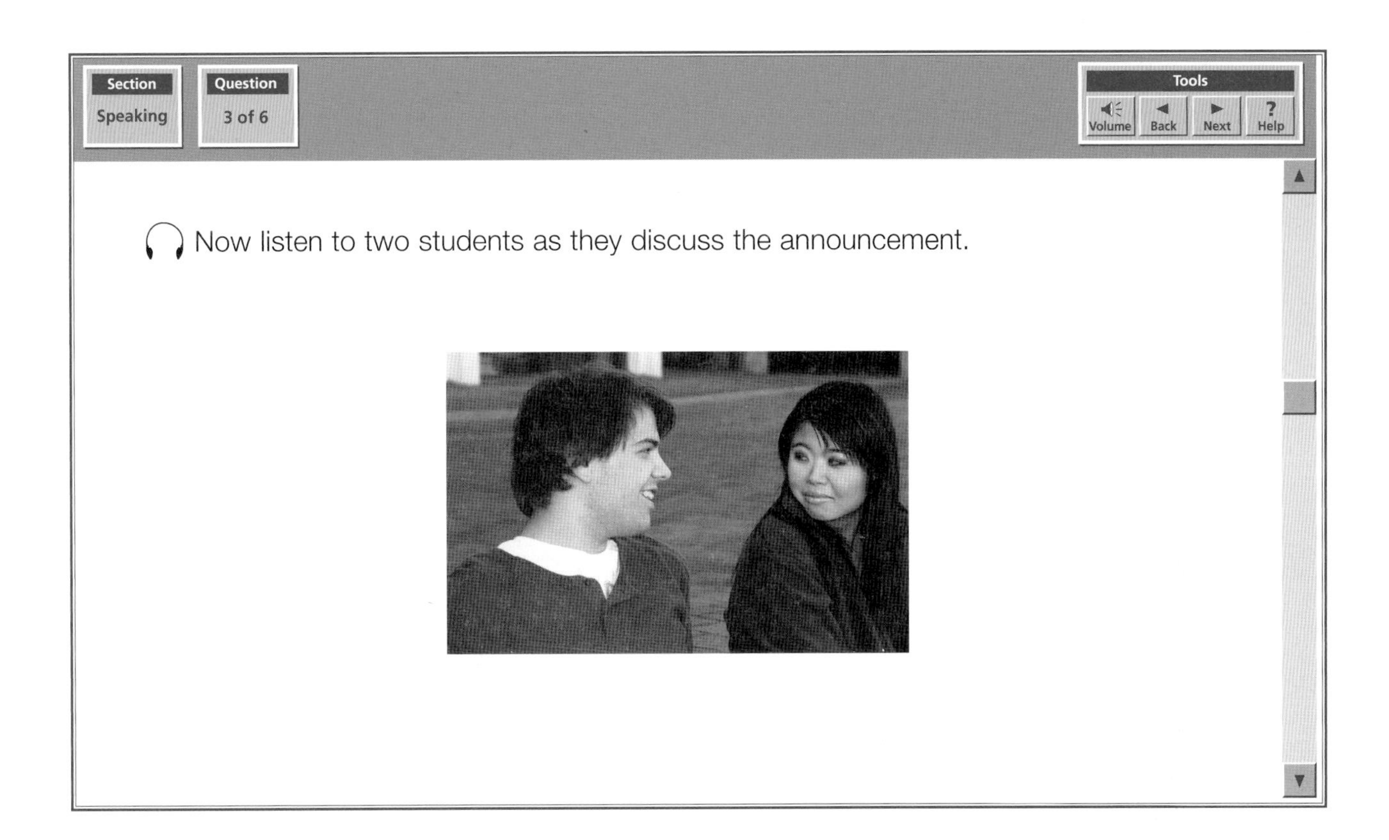
Section
Speaking
Question
3 of 6
Tools
Volume
Back
Next
Help
Now listen to two students as they discuss the announcement.

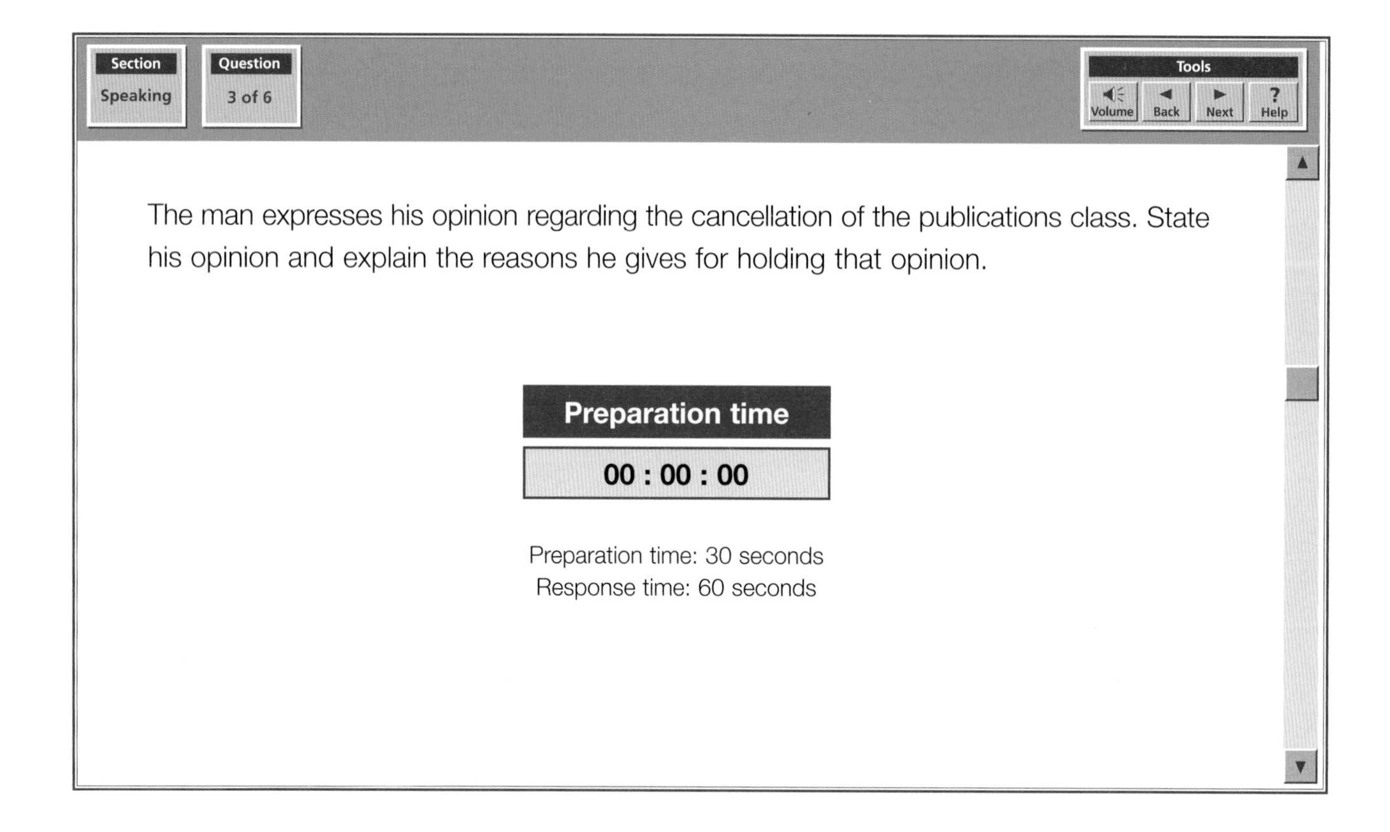
Section
Speaking
Question
3 of 6
Tools
Volume
Back
Next
Help
The man expresses his opinion regarding the cancellation of the publications class. State his opinion and explain the reasons he gives for holding that opinion.
Preparation time
00 : 00 : 00
Preparation time: 30 seconds
Response time: 60 seconds

Question 4 Track 92

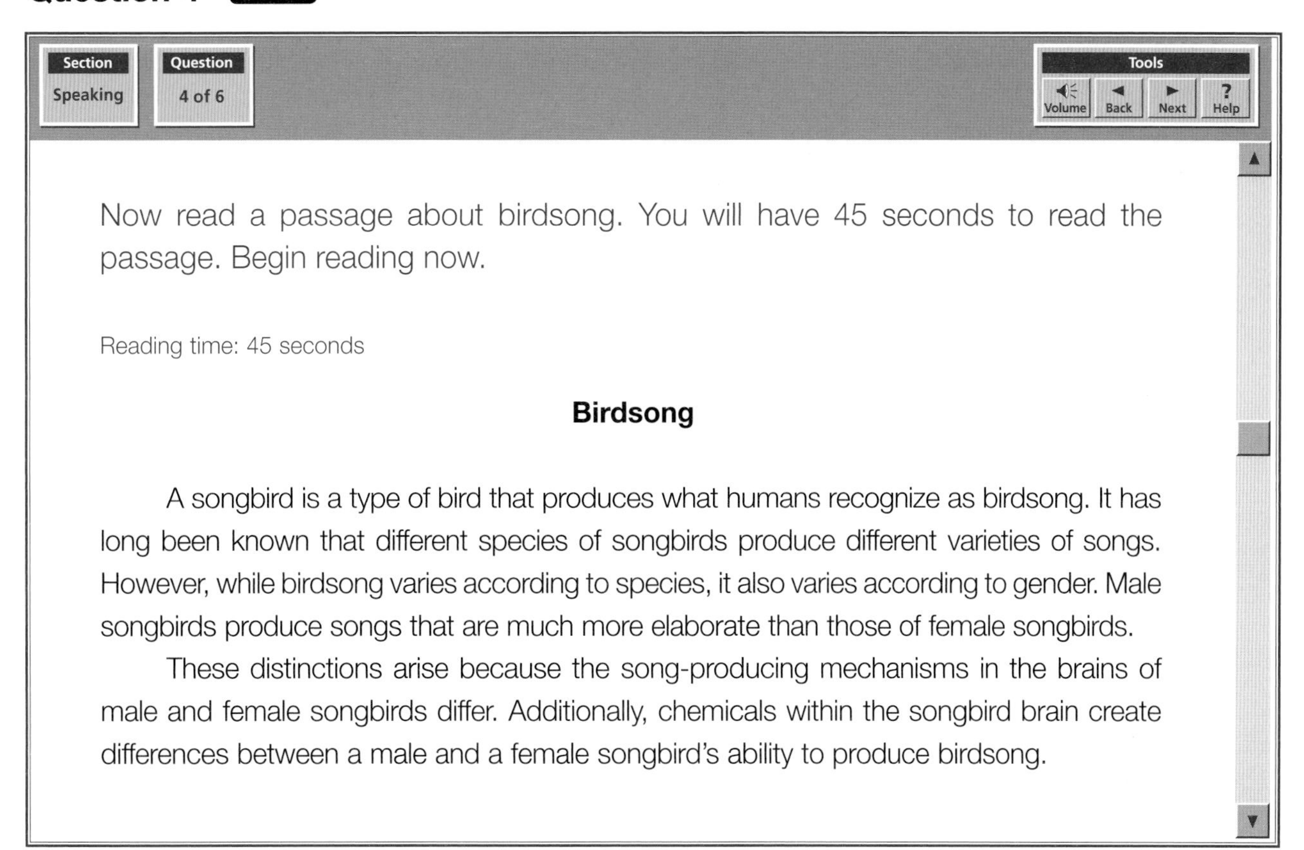

Now read a passage about birdsong. You will have 45 seconds to read the passage. Begin reading now.

Reading time: 45 seconds

Birdsong

A songbird is a type of bird that produces what humans recognize as birdsong. It has long been known that different species of songbirds produce different varieties of songs. However, while birdsong varies according to species, it also varies according to gender. Male songbirds produce songs that are much more elaborate than those of female songbirds.

These distinctions arise because the song-producing mechanisms in the brains of male and female songbirds differ. Additionally, chemicals within the songbird brain create differences between a male and a female songbird's ability to produce birdsong.

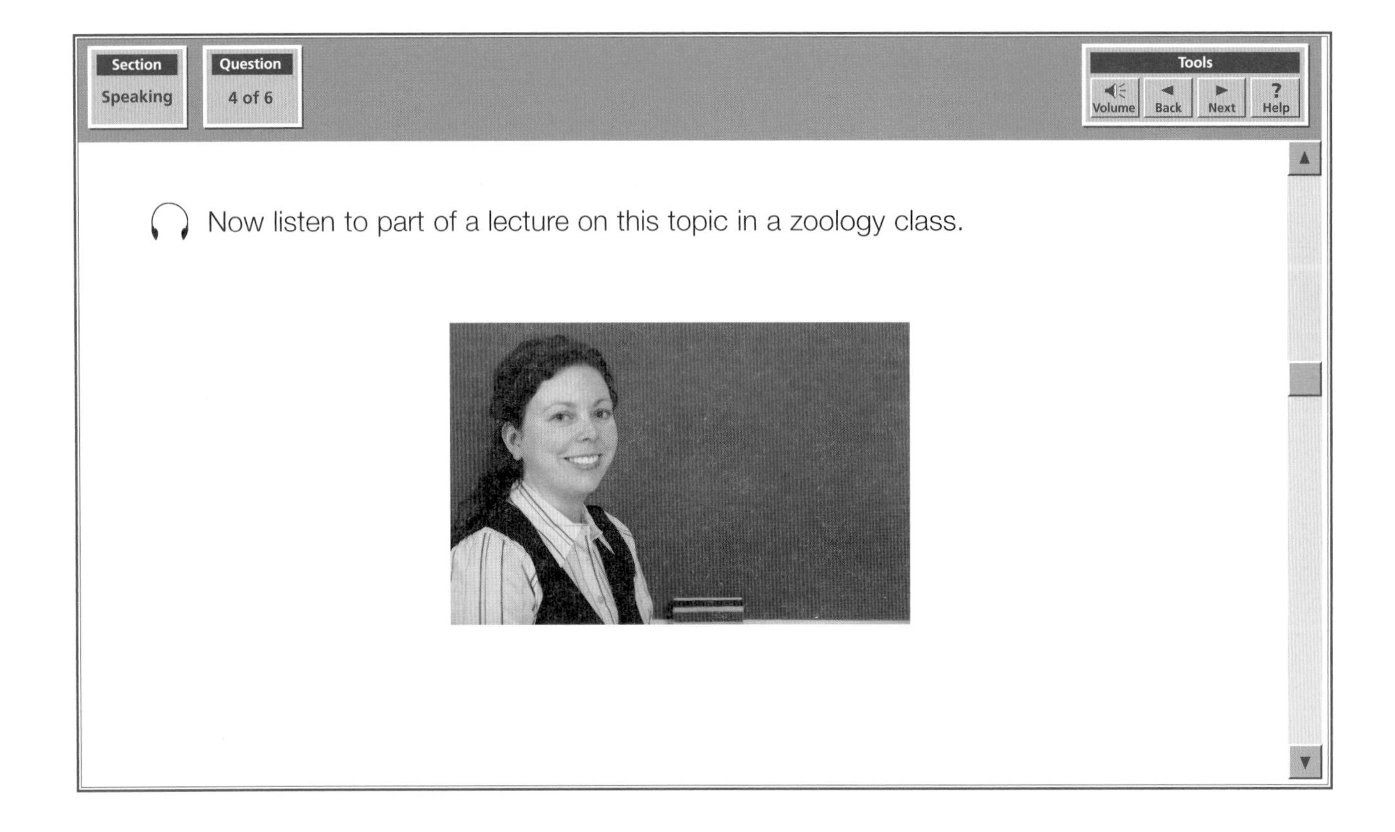
Section
Speaking
Question
4 of 6
Tools
Volume
Back
Next
Help
Now listen to part of a lecture on this topic in a zoology class.

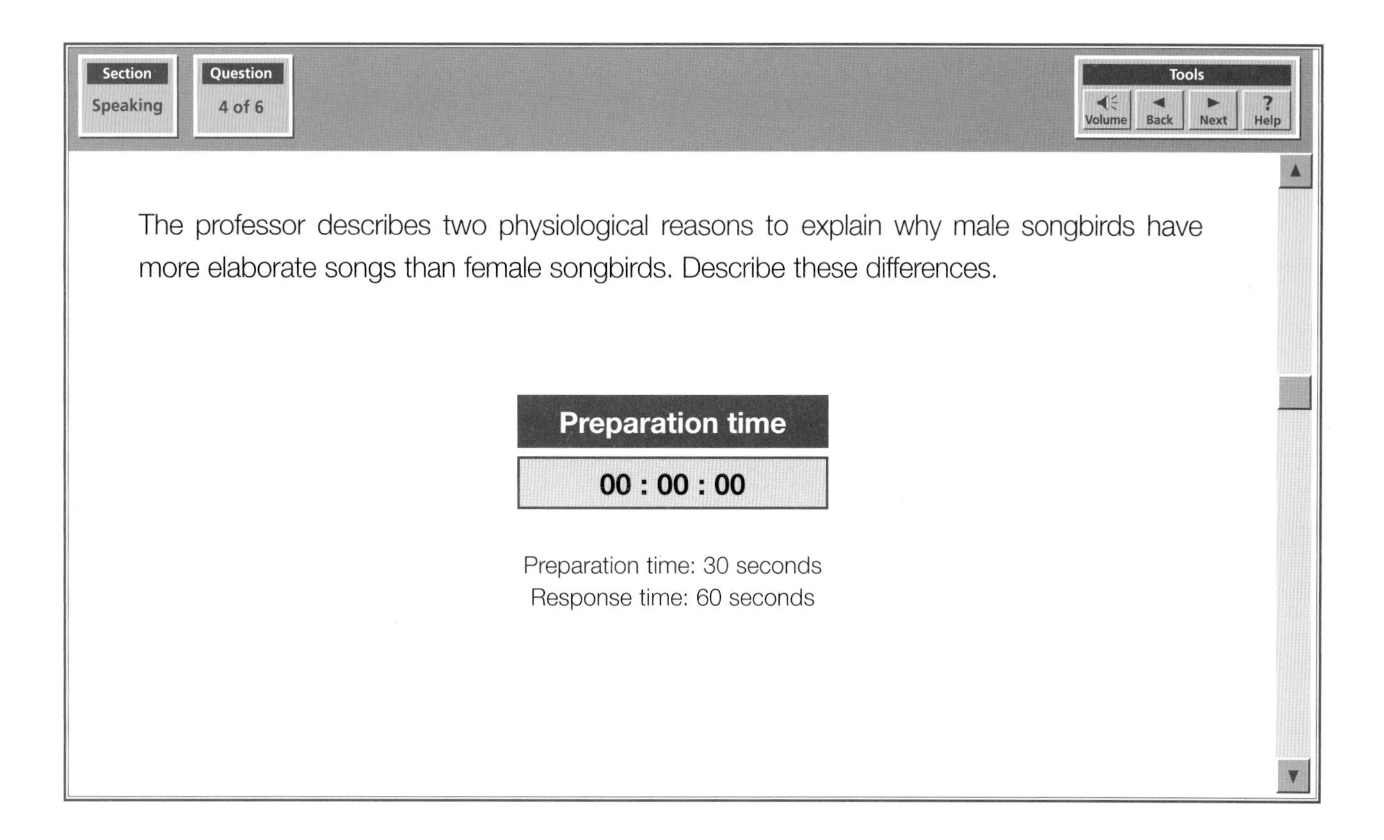
Section
Speaking
Question
4 of 6
Tools
Volume
Back
Next
Help
The professor describes two physiological reasons to explain why male songbirds have more elaborate songs than female songbirds. Describe these differences.
Preparation time
00 : 00 : 00
Preparation time: 30 seconds
Response time: 60 seconds

Question 5 Track 93

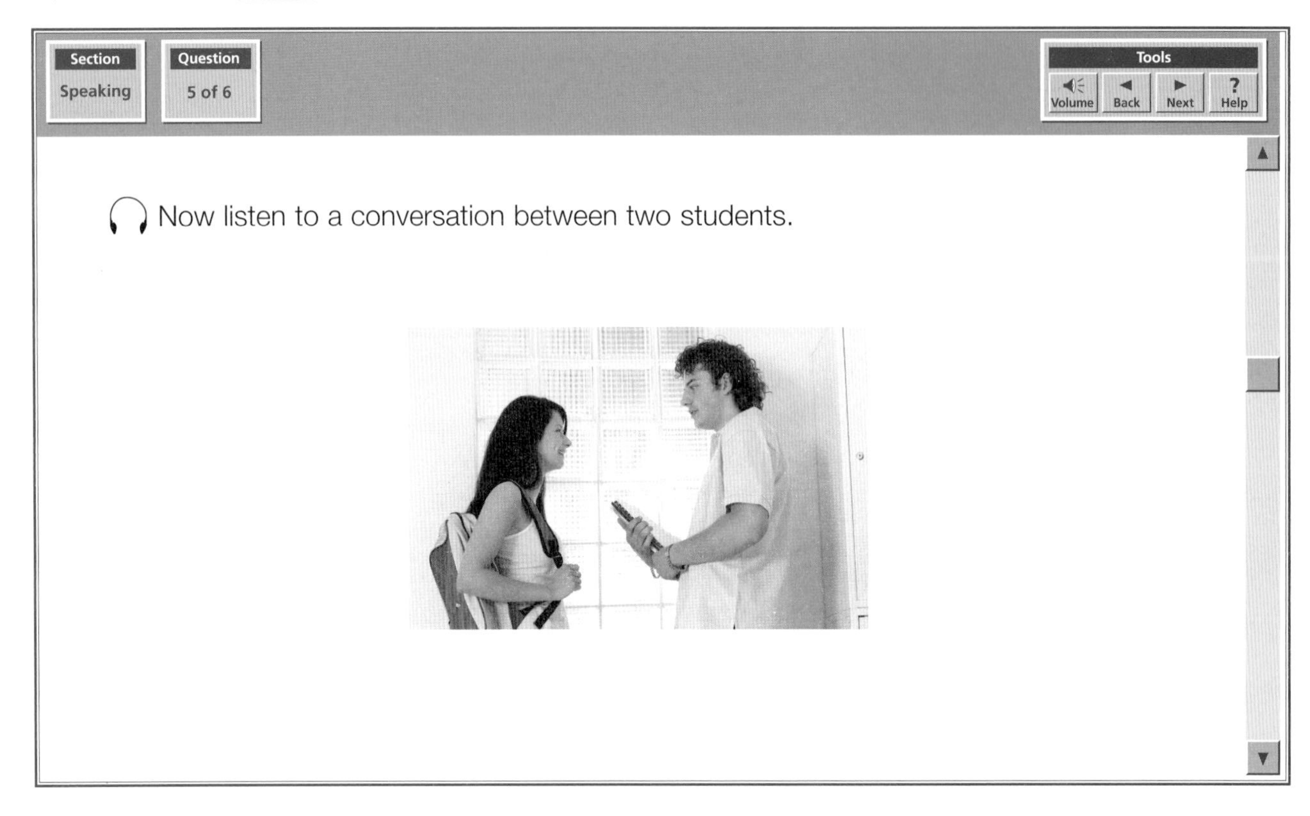

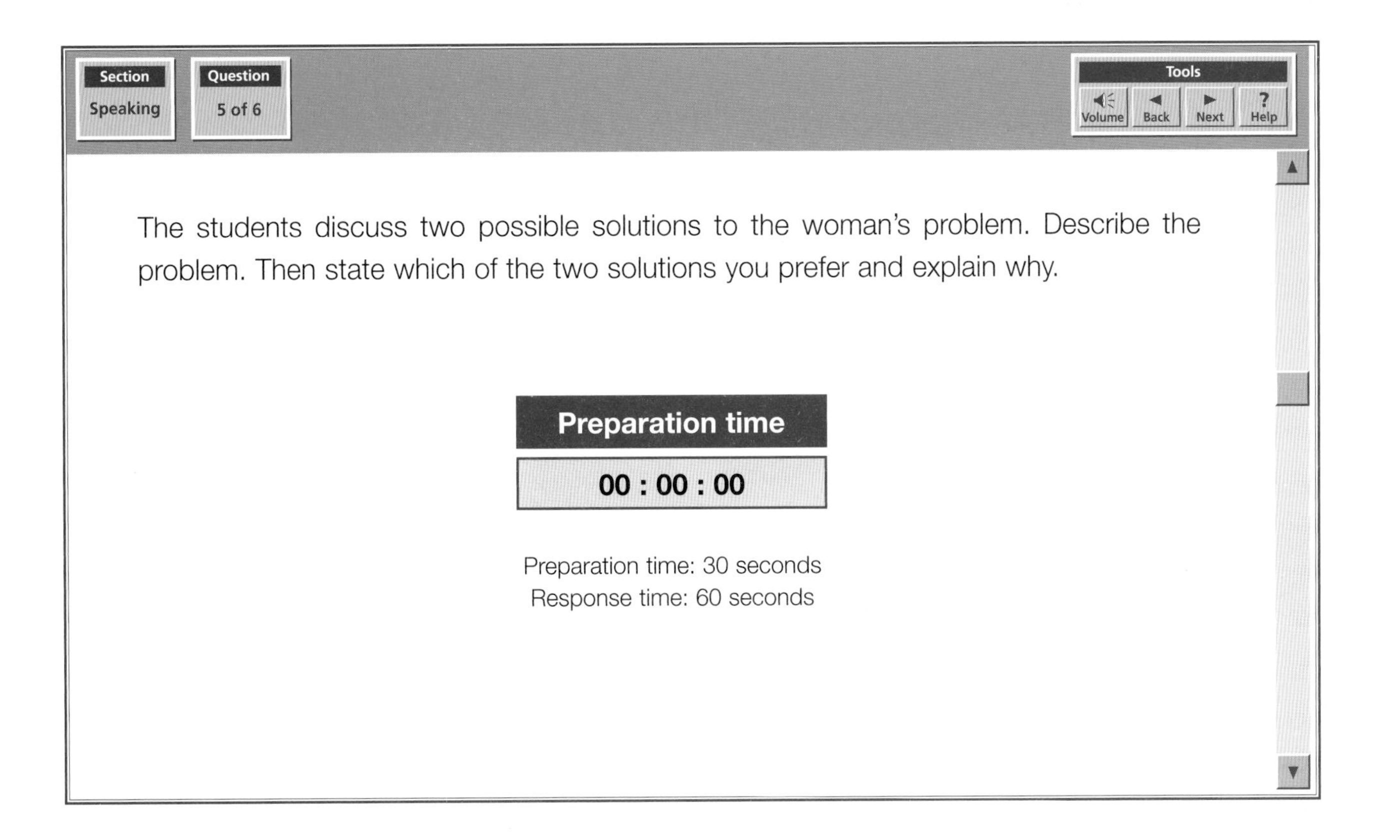
Section
Speaking
Question
5 of 6
Tools
Volume
Back
Next
Help
The students discuss two possible solutions to the woman's problem. Describe the problem. Then state which of the two solutions you prefer and explain why.
Preparation time
00 : 00 : 00
Preparation time: 30 seconds
Response time: 60 seconds

Question 6 **Track 94**

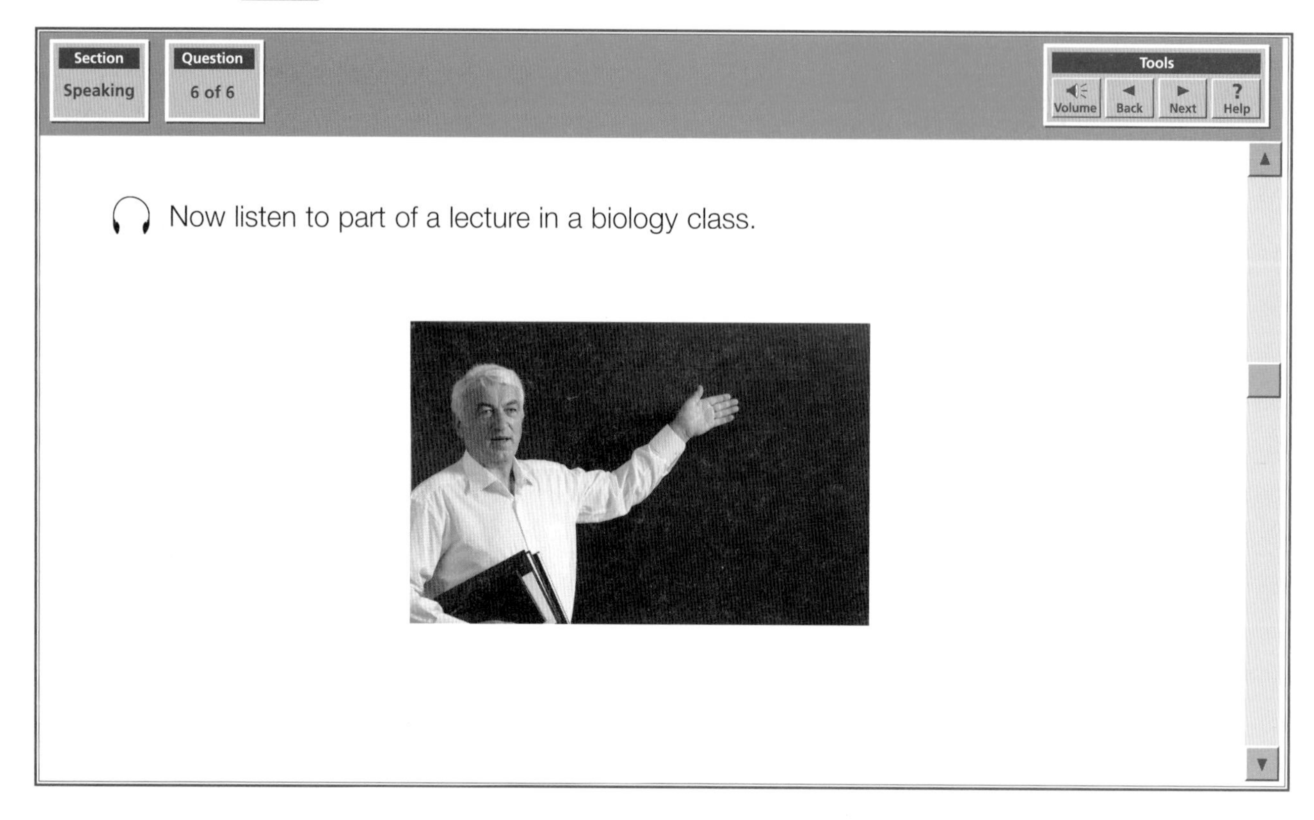

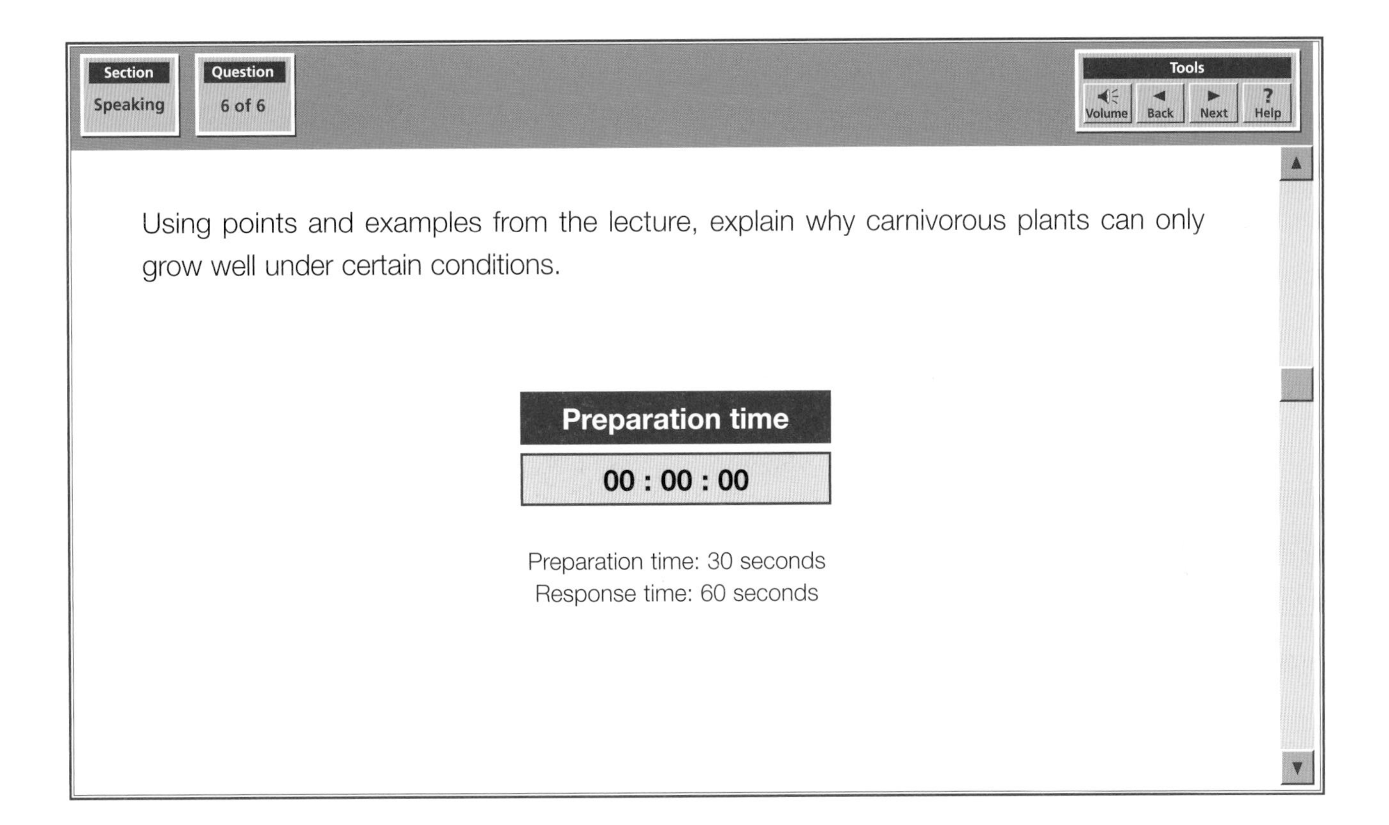
Section
Speaking
Question
6 of 6
Tools
Volume
Back
Next
Help
Using points and examples from the lecture, explain why carnivorous plants can only grow well under certain conditions.
Preparation time
00 : 00 : 00
Preparation time: 30 seconds
Response time: 60 seconds

Transcripts

Part 1

Chapter 1 Organizing Speech

Q1 Practice 1

▸ Step 2 - Sample Response

A fascinating city that I visited in my past was Jerusalem in Israel. I enjoyed myself there because my family originated from Israel. I had always wanted to see the place from where my ancestors came. By traveling there, I was able to witness firsthand the culture of my ancestors. I also enjoyed visiting Jerusalem because I had never visited an area before with so much history. Many of the buildings and places in Israel date back thousands of years. These ancient areas captivated me, and I loved exploring them.

Q1 Practice 2

▸ Step 2 - Sample Response

For my career, I would choose to be a wildlife photographer. I would prefer this job because I have always been fascinated with how wild animals behave in their natural environments. Photographing them would allow me to observe many different species and capture their behavior up close. Such a career would also enable me to travel to remote parts of the world. I would get to visit a diverse range of natural habitats and observe wildlife in places where most people never go. The experiences that I would encounter would be vast and exciting.

Q1 Practice 3

▸ Step 2 - Sample Response

A bad situation recently taught me that staying safe is more important than obtaining a goal. I learned this while climbing a peak with a group of friends a couple of weekends ago. We wanted to get to the top so badly that we kept going even though the weather became worse. We made it to the summit. However, by the time we turned around, a blizzard had come in. When we finally got back to camp, we were freezing and exhausted. I learned that some goals are not worth the risk of getting injured.

Q2 Practice 1

▸ Step 2 - Sample Responses

Opinion 1

I would prefer to live somewhere that is near the mountains. Then I could go for long hikes and backpacking trips. I enjoy going for hikes in the mountains with my group of friends. It is very rewarding to get to the top of a peak and look out over the city below. In addition, I would be able to go downhill skiing as much as I wanted during the winter. Skiing is one of my favorite sports, and I think I would be miserable spending a winter away from the slopes.

Opinion 2

I would prefer to live somewhere that is near the ocean. Then I could learn how to sail, which has been my lifelong dream. When I was little, my uncle took me out on his sail boat and ever since, I have always wanted to sail my own boat by myself. It is very peaceful drifting out among the waves. In addition, I would not ever have to endure harsh winters or snowstorms. I want to stay in a place with mild winters, and maritime climates are generally warmer than alpine climates.

Q2 Practice 2

▸ Step 2 - Sample Responses

Opinion 1

I prefer to have just a few close friends rather than many friends. First of all, I think it is important to build strong relationships with your friends, and it is difficult to do that when you have a large number of friends. In my experience, the best friendships I have formed are with those few people that I have gotten to know very well. Secondly, I think having lots of friends can be overwhelming. When I have lots of friends around, I find it hard to divide my time between so many people and still have time for myself and schoolwork.

Opinion 2

I prefer to have many friends rather than just a few close ones. First of all, I think it is fun to get to know lots of people, and there is always someone to talk to when you have many friends. In my experience, I have always felt like I had more support available when I had more friends to consult. Secondly, I think having only a few close friends can make you feel isolated. When I am around lots of friends, on the other hand, I find that I am better able to reach out to others and experience many different things.

Q2 Practice 3

▸ Step 2 - Sample Responses

Opinion 1

I would prefer to work and make money in the summer. This would give me spending money during the school year to go on trips with my friends. For example, last semester, my friends and I took a spring break trip to Europe. It was a remarkable experience, and I could not have afforded it if I had not worked throughout my summer vacation. Also, if I do not have a job during this period, I often get bored. I would rather keep busy at a job earning money than sit around at home with nothing to do.

Opinion 2

I would prefer to take the summer off. This would give me time to rest after a busy school year. For example, last year I worked so hard during the school year that I often did not get enough sleep. It is nice to have a summer where I can sleep late and recuperate. Also, if I do not have to work during this period, then I have time to do things I enjoy. I would rather hang out with my friends, go swimming, and read novels than go to the same job every day.

Chapter 2 Synthesizing Information

Q3 Practice 1

▸ Step 2 - Conversation

W: Have you heard that they're no longer going to provide us with printer paper in the lab?

M: Yeah, that's too bad. You use the lab all the time to print out your papers, don't you?

W: Yeah, I don't know anyone who prints out stuff that's not school-related. My friends and I are always printing out drafts of research papers or journal articles. I don't understand where the university got this idea that students don't use the printers for schoolwork.

M: Yeah, I have no idea. But at least this'll let them save money to buy more computers. Now more students can use the lab.

W: Maybe, but I'm not so sure. I think lots of students are going to stop using the computers. They won't want to use the lab if they have to bring their own paper.

M: Yeah. That is a hassle.

W: And you remember that lab fee we have to pay at the beginning of the semester? Students aren't going to pay it when they don't use the lab. Which means less money for stuff like new computers.

M: You've got a point, there.

▸ Step 4 - Sample Response

The announcement says that students must use their own paper to print from the computer lab starting at the end of the month. The woman does not agree with the university's decision. First, she thinks that the university is wrong to conclude that students print materials unrelated to school work. Everyone she knows prints scholarly materials at the lab's printers. Secondly, she thinks using the money saved on printer paper to buy new computers is not a good idea. She feels that fewer students will want to use the lab if they are forced to bring their own printing paper. Therefore, they will not want to pay the lab fees at the beginning of the semester, which means less money for the school to purchase new computers with.

Q3 Practice 2

▸ Step 2 - Conversation

M: Wow, did you see this announcement?

W: Yeah, they're raising the price of parking tickets from $35 to $50. That's a pretty substantial jump, wouldn't you say?

M: Maybe, but I think the change is long overdue. There's definitely a serious problem with students parking alongside the street, not just near fire lanes but also in front of all those shops near campus. I'm sure it's bad for business because it prevents customers from parking there.

W: Yeah, I hadn't thought of that. It would be nice for customers if more spots were available close to the stores.

M: It'd also be great if campus security could make enough money from parking tickets to build a new lot closer to school. The current one is just too far away. It often takes me a half hour to get to class.

W: I know what you mean. It takes me a while, too. I don't know why the university just didn't build a parking lot closer to campus.

M: But now hopefully they'll get the chance to fix that. Then students won't have to waste so much time walking to class.

▶ **Step 4 - Sample Response**

The announcement says that the price of parking tickets will be raised from $35 to $50. The man supports the decision because he agrees that the university has a problem with students parking alongside the street. He thinks that by parking in front of shops near campus, students are hurting the businesses because they are preventing customers from parking there. He also thinks that raising money to build a new parking lot close to campus is a good idea because the current lot is too far away. It takes him a half hour to get to class. If the lot was closer, students would not have to spend a lot of time walking to class from their cars.

Q3 Practice 3

▶ **Step 2 - Conversation**

M: Too bad they won't be providing paper copies of the course catalogue anymore.

W: Why's that a problem? It'll be posted online. And the university will be saving money because they won't have to pay for printing costs.

M: Yeah, but there are plenty of other ways the university could save money. For instance, they could send out emails instead of posting announcements like these.

W: True, but registering online is more convenient for students. It'll be easy to just log onto the school network and sign up for classes whenever you've got the time.

M: I disagree. I think it's going to be highly inconvenient.

W: I don't see how.

M: Not everyone's great at using a computer. And many students are going to have to learn how to navigate through the computer catalogue, which will be a challenge. Paper-based catalogues are much simpler to use.

W: Well, all right. I suppose you have a point. It is pretty easy to just flip through a paper catalogue.

M: Exactly. I bet the registrar's going to be overwhelmed with students who are having problems with this new catalogue system.

▶ **Step 4 - Sample Response**

The announcement says that the university will replace paper copies of the course catalogue with an online catalogue. The man thinks that this is a bad decision. He feels that the university can save money in other ways, like sending email announcements instead of posting them. The man also thinks the online catalogues will be more inconvenient. He mentions that it will not be easy for students to use computers to register for classes. Many will have trouble navigating through a computer-based catalogue. He believes that paper catalogues are much easier to figure out. He concludes by saying that a lot of students will have to visit the registrar anyway because they will have problems with the new system.

Q4 Practice 1

▶ **Step 2 - Lecture**

M: Color psychology isn't just for psychologists. Regular people use color all the time to portray or influence particular moods. Colors can be separated into two types—warm colors and cool colors—based on how they influence people. I'll give you a few examples of how they're used to achieve desired effects.

Warm colors—like pinks and oranges—induce feelings of comfort. Now, in some countries, school sports teams paint certain locker rooms pink. Do you know why? Well, many sports teams paint their opponents' locker rooms pink in hopes that it will be so comforting that it will cause the opposing players to lose energy. After all, you don't want to be comforted before an important game. You should be excited and ready for action if you're going to play well. Hence, this is a good example of how color is used to manipulate others.

Now, since cool colors make people feel confident, blue is a common clothing color for people like policemen and others in positions of authority. It's a color that's considered to be powerful without seeming menacing. It's no coincidence that blue suits are a popular choice to wear to job interviews, and actually, fashion consultants recommend wearing blue to interviews or new jobs because it serves as an outward display of confidence.

▶ **Step 4 - Sample Response**

The reading mentions that there are two types of color—warm colors like pink and red, and cool colors like blue. It says that warm colors cause people to feel warm and comforted, while cool colors inspire confidence. The professor then gives examples of how these colors can be used to influence mood. The professor mentions how sports teams often paint their opponents' locker rooms the warm color, pink. They do this in hopes that the pink color will be so comforting that their opponents will lose energy. The professor then mentions that people are often advised to wear blue suits to job interviews and new jobs so that they seem more confident.

Q4 Practice 2

▸ Step 2 - Lecture

W: A baboon is one type of animal that uses a highly structured dominance hierarchy. Let's take a closer look at just how baboons use dominance hierarchies within their social groups.

First off, dominance hierarchies in the baboon species are used to keep the group organized and stable. This is done through a ranking system. Each baboon in the group has a specific rank. Those in lower ranks follow the leadership of those in higher ranks. For example, baboons in a group follow the leadership of a dominant male. This individual makes major group decisions—like where to find food—and the lower ranked members follow his lead. This allows dominant individuals to make quick decisions about what's best for the entire group, which could mean the difference between survival and death.

Dominance hierarchies also allow baboons to settle disputes over scarce resources. This is important for baboons that live on the African savanna. On the savanna, food is often scarce. Therefore, a dominant individual exists who can manage aggression and determine how food is distributed. However, baboons that live in the forest have a more relaxed dominance hierarchy because food is more available. Conflicts over food are less likely to occur here, so the role of the dominant male in forest baboon groups is not as clearly defined as that of a savanna baboon's.

▸ Step 4 - Sample Response

The reading says that dominance hierarchies exist to maintain order and resolve conflicts in animal groups. The professor discusses how baboons use dominance hierarchies to maintain order through a ranking system. There is a dominant male baboon in each group, and the lesser ranked baboons follow what he does. The professor then says that dominance hierarchies help baboons manage conflicts over scarce resources. This is important for baboons on the savanna because food is rarer. Therefore, according to the professor, a strong dominant leader needs to be in control to manage resources and aggression. Conversely, the professor explains that the role of the dominant male in forest baboon groups is less defined because food there is more common.

Q4 Practice 3

▸ Step 2 - Lecture

M: Wegener first noticed that the continents seemed to fit together like a jigsaw puzzle. When you look at a map of the world, you can see a fit between the eastern coast of South America and the western coast of Africa. But this realization wasn't enough to prove his hypothesis of continental drift. However, scientists have found additional evidence which proves that Wegener's hypothesis is accurate.

One type of evidence involves fossil records. Scientists have found fossils of ancient animals distributed widely across the continents, indicating that the land masses must have been joined at some point in prehistory. For instance, fossil remains of one of the first marine reptiles, known as Mesosaurus, have been found in both South America and Africa. This suggests that Africa and South America were once part of the same continent.

It's also true that the geology of the South American and African coasts is remarkably similar, lending further evidence to Wegener's hypothesis. When you fit the two continents together, you can see that distinct rock formations and mineral deposits match up. For example, the same type of sandstone hills that end on the west coast of Africa can be found on the east coast of South America. This same type of sandstone occurs nowhere else in the world so clearly. Obviously, these continents were connected at one time.

▸ Step 4 - Sample Response

The passage first defines continental drift, which says that the continents were once one landmass that broke apart and are now drifting away from each other. It states that evidence of continental drift can be found through fossils and rock formations. The professor explains how scientists have come across fossils of an ancient marine reptile in both South America and South Africa. This led scientists to believe that the two continents must have been joined at one time. The professor also states that scientists have found that the coasts of both continents have similar sandstone rock formations and mineral types. This further supports the hypothesis that these formations were at one time connected on a single continent.

Chapter 3 Stating Opinions and Summarizing

Q5 Practice 1

▸ Step 1 - Conversation

M: You all right, Jess? You look upset.

W: Oh hi, Dave. Yeah, I just checked my semester grade online. I have a C right now in my organic chemistry class.

M: A C isn't so bad.

W: Yes, but I have to maintain a B average to keep my scholarship.

M: Oh. So what're you going to do?

W: I don't know. I really need this class for my major.

M: Can you just request to take the class as a pass or fail?

W: What is that again?

M: It means all you have to do is pass the class. It'll show up on your transcript as a pass. However, it won't list a specific grade. Therefore, it won't affect your GPA at all.

W: Oh yes, now I remember. The problem is, pass or fail grades don't help improve your GPA either. If I ace this upcoming midterm, I could raise my grade in this class to an A-. That would matter if I choose to take this class as a pass or fail.

M: So basically, if you can ace this next test, you can raise your grade?

W: Exactly.

M: Well, they have free tutoring sessions through the library. Why don't you get a tutor to help you?

W: That's an option. But I'm still not sure if they'll be able to help me to understand the material. It's complicated stuff to learn. Plus, I'm usually really busy with my job and other classes.

▸ Step 3 - Sample Responses

Opinion 1

The woman is currently getting a C in her organic chemistry class. She needs to improve her grade to keep her scholarship. The man suggests that she either request to take the class as a pass or fail or that she go to tutoring sessions. I think the first option is best. Since she is already busy with work and other classes, adding tutoring sessions to her busy schedule might make her fall behind in other areas. This could end up hurting her GPA even more. Also, if she takes the class as a pass or fail, it will not affect her GPA at all. It will not matter if she gets a C in the class. This will relieve some of the pressure the girl feels.

Opinion 2

The woman is currently getting a C in her organic chemistry class. She needs to improve her grade to keep her scholarship. The man suggests that she either request to take the class as a pass or fail or that she go to tutoring sessions. I think the second option is best. Since she is having trouble with the class, I think it would be worthwhile to schedule study time with tutors who can help her prepare for the tests. This could help her learn the material really well. Also, if she does well on the next test, she might get a good grade in the class. It could raise her GPA. This will not happen, however, if she takes the class as a pass or fail.

Q5 Practice 2

▸ Step 1 - Conversation

W: Hey, Will, are you excited for the field trip next weekend for Professor O'Leary's geology class to the mountains?

M: Yeah, I was. But I just found out that my grandfather is in the hospital. My mom and I are flying out to go visit him tomorrow. So I don't think we'll be back in time for me to go on the trip. What time are you leaving again?

W: We're all leaving from the student parking lot at nine a.m. on Friday.

M: I thought so. I won't be back in town until Friday afternoon. So I won't be able to leave with the class.

W: You do know that this class is a big portion of our grade?

M: I know, but I don't know what else to do.

W: Well, can you catch up with us all on Saturday morning? You know, drive out there by yourself and meet up with us in the mountains.

M: I guess so. The drive's not too long, but I don't know the area. I'm afraid I won't be able to find the rest of the class.

W: Well, we'll be on the mountain trail. There's lots of trail signs up there. But I can sympathize with you. I'd be anxious about getting lost, too. Could you explain the situation to Professor O'Leary? Maybe he'd give you an extra credit assignment to make up for it.

M: Possibly. However, I'm not sure if he'll agree to that or not.

▸ Step 3 - Sample Responses

Opinion 1

The man has to visit his grandfather in the hospital, and he will not be back in time to go on a field trip with his class on Friday. The trip is a big part of his grade. The woman suggests that he either meet up with the class Saturday morning or ask the professor for an alternative assignment. I think it would be better for him to catch up with the group on Saturday. Since there are lots of signs to help him find out where to go, he should be able to locate the class easily. Also, he will not have to worry about whether or not the professor will allow him to do an alternative assignment. It is too risky to depend solely on the professor's kindness.

Opinion 2

The man has to visit his grandfather in the hospital, and he will not be back in time to go on a field trip with his class on Friday. The trip is a big part of his grade. The woman suggests that he either meet up with the class Saturday morning or ask the professor for an alternative assignment. I think it would be better for him to ask his professor for an alternative assignment. Since this is an emergency, his professor will probably allow him to do another assignment. Also, the man will not have to worry about getting lost. It is too risky to try and find his way around as he does not know the area well.

Q5 Practice 3

▸ Step 1 - Conversation

M: So, have you applied for student housing yet for next year?

W: Yeah, I applied to live in the West dorms. What about you?

M: I haven't applied yet. I'm having trouble with the costs. I just don't have enough money left over to afford to live on campus. But I have to find some way to live in the dorms.

W: Do you have any ideas on how to raise the money?

M: That's what I'm worried about. I can't get a regular job because I have a heavy course load. My schedule's really busy.

W: Have you thought about getting a work-study job?

M: A work-study job?

W: Yeah. It's where you work for the university. In exchange, they'll pay off some of your living expenses.

M: Oh, yeah. I know some people who do that.

W: The best thing is, their hours are really flexible. You could probably work it around your heavy class schedule.

M: Hmm . . . that's definitely an option. I'd still have to work, though. I don't know if I can manage both work and school.

W: Or you could always take out a loan. That way you wouldn't have to worry about working at all. You could just concentrate on school.

M: That's true. Of course, then I'd have to worry about paying it back after I finished school. That's a lot of debt.

W: Well, you'll just have to decide what will work best for you.

▸ Step 3 - Sample Responses

Opinion 1

The woman needs to live on campus to go to school, but she cannot afford to live in the dorms. The man suggests that she get a work-study job or that she take out a loan. I think she should get a work-study job. It will be better to pay costs off now than later, in my opinion. This option will give the woman the money to live on campus without going into debt. She will not have to worry about paying back a loan when she graduates. In addition, with a work-study job, she will be able to work around her own schedule. This way, the woman will not have to worry about missing class or getting behind on her schoolwork.

Opinion 2

The woman needs to live on campus to go to school, but she can't afford to live in the dorms. The man suggests that she get a work-study job or that she take out a loan. I think she should take out a loan. It will give her the money to live on campus without having to work. This option will allow the woman to concentrate more on her schoolwork. She will not have the added stress of maintaining a job and a heavy course load. In addition, taking out a loan will also allow her to pay for housing at the beginning of the semester. This way, she will not have to wait until she gets money from working during the school year.

Q6 Practice 1

▸ Step 1 - Lecture

M: Today I want to talk about minimalism—a prominent movement in American and European art—which emerged around the 1960s. The idea of minimalism was to reduce a work of art to its minimum number of colors, shapes, lines, and textures. Minimalist artists resisted the traditional idea that art had to represent an object or an experience. Instead, they created paintings and sculptures that were unique objects unto themselves—objects that didn't stand for something else. To achieve this effect, minimalist artists used two design techniques in their art.

First, they tended to use materials that were uniform in shape. Take, for instance, Carl Andre's 1969 sculpture "Steel Zinc Plain." This is a perfect example of how minimalist artists chose the simplest, most uniform shapes to piece together a work of art. Andre uses one of the very simplest of geometric structures: the square. He took square plates of zinc and square plates of steel and arranged them in a checkerboard pattern on the floor. So basically, he created what looked a giant checkerboard that could be walked over and stood upon.

Second, minimalist artists often used one kind of material in a repeating pattern. The 1966 piece by Dan Flavin called "Monument for V. Tatlin" clearly demonstrates the use of repetition. In this piece, Flavin uses only one type of material: a pre-made fluorescent tube—you know, those long, glowing tubes used for industrial lighting. He took several of these and arranged them into a miniature monument. The idea was inspired by the Russian artist Vladimir Tatlin's proposed design for a new revolving spiral monument that would be taller than the Eiffel Tower. But in the end, Flavin created a simple sculpture that was nothing like the traditional grandeur of a real monument.

▸ Step 3 - Sample Response

Minimalist artists reduced artwork to its basic colors and shapes. The professor says minimalist artists created simple, unique objects by using uniform materials and arranging lots of them in a repeating pattern. The first piece that the professor mentioned was as an example of how minimalists use uniform shapes. In his piece, the artist used square-shaped plates and arranged them in a checkerboard pattern that people can walk on. The second piece the professor mentioned was an example of how minimalists use repetition. For his piece, the artist took several fluorescent tubes and arranged them into a simple miniature tower. This miniature tower was inspired by plans for a grand new monument.

Q6 Practice 2

▸ Step 1 - Lecture

M: There are many theories out there about what it takes to be an effective leader, but the one attribute that links all these theories together is charisma. Charisma is the ability to inspire enthusiasm, interest, or affection in other people. So basically, the theory of charismatic leadership assumes that all good leaders must have charisma in order to attract followers . . . and according to the theory, charismatic leaders share two common traits.

First of all, charismatic leaders create a compelling vision that appeals to their followers' values, interests, hopes, and dreams. A charismatic leader is not content simply to lead a group along its present course, but strives to reach high goals and ideals. In this sense, Dr. Martin Luther King Jr., a famous American during the 1960s, was a charismatic leader; his vision was this: that all men were created equal no matter their differences. He helped convince people that treating certain Americans unfairly was wrong and attracted a large number of followers who helped accomplish his vision. He was thus able to inspire the American government to pass laws that guaranteed certain rights for all people.

Secondly, charismatic leaders demonstrate their vision through action. They don't just delegate tasks and tell people how to behave, but rather exhibit ideal behavior through their own actions. There was a famous World War II general, named Patton, for example, who once demonstrated this approach to leadership by intervening at the scene of a traffic jam. He pulled up to the jam, and rather than yelling orders, he got out of his jeep and started directing traffic himself. As traffic started to move, he turned the job over to the military police. In this manner, Patton was able to teach his subordinates . . . in this case, the police . . . through action, and he also gained their admiration.

▸ Step 3 - Sample Response

The professor says that according to the theory of charismatic leadership, all leaders attract followers with charisma and share two common traits. One trait of a charismatic leader is the ability to create a vision that is appealing to his or her followers. The professor uses Dr. Martin Luther King Jr. as an example of a charismatic leader with a vision. His vision was that all people would be treated as equals. He helped convince the American government to pass laws giving everyone certain rights. The second trait of a charismatic leader is the ability to demonstrate vision through action. The professor uses General Patton as an example. He got rid of a traffic jam by directing traffic himself.

Q6 Practice 3

▸ Step 1 - Lecture

W: We would all like to think that we make decisions for ourselves—that we can resist things like advertisements and peer pressure. But as it turns out, the power of conformity—that is, the tendency to be influenced by others within a group—is much stronger than we might imagine. In the 1950s, the American social psychologist, Solomon Asch, showed just how much the pressure to conform can affect our decisions. He conducted an experiment which showed that not only are most people easily willing to conform to a group, they will also compromise their own knowledge to do so.

Asch's experiment involved nothing more than three straight black lines drawn on note cards. During the experiment, he asked a room full of students to announce out loud, one by one, their answers to a series of questions about the length of the three lines. They might be asked which line was longest, which two lines were of the same length, and so on. In reality, only the very last participant to state his answer was ignorant of what the experiment was about. The other students in the room had been previously informed to give the same incorrect answers to the questions, so when the last student's turn came to answer, he had to decide whether to go with the group's response or to trust what he saw with his own eyes.

Before Asch collected the results of his experiment, he believed that people would stand up against group pressure, that they wouldn't sacrifice their own truths to go along with the crowd. Turns out he was wrong. His results showed that a third of the people tested gave the same answer as everyone else in the room, even though it contradicted the truth they saw before them.

▸ Step 3 - Sample Response

The professor says Asch did an experiment which showed that the pressure to conform to a group greatly influences the decisions that people make. For his experiment, he used cards with black lines drawn on them and asked students to answer questions about the lines out loud. All the students but the last one was told to give the same wrong answer. Asch found that a third of the time, the last student gave the same answer as the rest of the group, even though it was different from what that student had observed. Asch's experiment showed that people are often willing to sacrifice what they know to be true in order to conform to a group.

Part 2

Chapter 4 Test Questions 1 and 2

Q1 Practice 1

▸ Step 3 - Sample Response

My favorite place to go to in my city is the huge park downtown. I love going there because it is a great place to watch people doing various activities. For instance, I can watch people jogging, couples walking their dogs, or children playing at the playground. It is fun to see how they all interact with each other. Also, I enjoy going to the park because I can almost always find someone to play volleyball with. This game is a great way to meet new friends, get some exercise, and take a break from schoolwork.

Q1 Practice 2

▸ Step 3 - Sample Response

As a child, one of my favorite books was *Where the Wild Things Are*. It is about a boy who uses his imagination to turn his room into a wild forest where he becomes the king of the Wild Things. I liked the book mostly because of its great pictures. Even though the Wild Things are supposed to be fearsome monsters, they are actually quite comical in the pictures. I also liked the book because the story was simple and easy to memorize. I felt proud because I could recite the story even before I knew how to read.

Q1 Practice 3

▸ Step 2 - Sample Response

One teacher who has positively impacted my life was my ninth-grade literature teacher, Ms. Murphy. She helped me to develop a passion for literature. Before her class, I never thought of actively pursuing literature as a course of study. However, Ms. Murphy's lectures made literature so much fun that I decided to study literature in college. Also, Ms. Murphy taught me how to deal with conflicts. Whenever she had a problem, she always handled it rationally rather than losing her temper. By following her example, I was able to handle conflicts better in my own life.

Q1 Practice 4

▸ Step 2 - Sample Response

The best advice I have ever received was from my mother. My mother advised me as a young child to take my schoolwork very seriously because it would help me in the future. It turned out to be the best advice that I have ever received. First, concentrating on my schoolwork helped me to achieve good grades, eventually allowing me to receive a college scholarship. I could not have afforded college without it. Plus, my good study habits throughout college enabled me to graduate at the top of my class. I was immediately eligible for all sorts of jobs.

Q2 Practice 1

▸ Step 3 - Sample Response

I would prefer to attend a local college. This way, if I encountered any problems, my family would be nearby to provide assistance. In high school, when I was doing poorly in a class, they were there to give me the advice I needed to pass it. I would want their support in college, also. Secondly, I think I would receive as good an education at a local college as at a national college, at half the cost. I know many graduates of less expensive local colleges who have attained even more success than those from prestigious universities.

Q2 Practice 2

▸ Step 3 - Sample Response

I prefer to visit educational places when I travel to new areas. Primarily, I like visiting educational places like museums because I am often curious about the area and the people I am visiting. I think that knowing the history and culture of a place helps me to better understand and appreciate it. I also enjoy visiting educational places because they are often distinctive to an area. In contrast, places for entertainment like movie theaters or amusement parks can generally be found anywhere. Since I can visit places like those at home, I would rather spend my time at places I will not see again.

Q2 Practice 3

▸ Step 2 - Sample Response

I firmly believe that parents should be permitted to influence the type of materials that children learn in schools. My first reason for this is because parents are often the best judges of what their children are ready to learn. They are also best aware of the areas in which their children are struggling. Parents' opinions about what their children should learn can be helpful for developing a curriculum. Secondly, children often feel uncomfortable talking to teachers about problems they have with materials. Consequently, it is important that their parents are able to intervene and speak for them.

Q2 Practice 4

▸ Step 2 - Sample Response

In spite of today's busy world, I do not think that it is a good idea for people to be constantly active. Being active all the time drains us of our energy. Our bodies need rest just like they need food in order to function properly. It is important to set aside time to relax and recharge our minds and bodies. Such a busy lifestyle is also counterproductive. Some people believe that by constantly being active, they are getting more done. However, in reality, I think we tend to get things done more efficiently when we take breaks between activities.

Chapter 5 Test Questions 3 and 4

Q3 Practice 1

▸ Step 1 - Conversation

M: What do you think about that announcement from the English Department? Do you think it's fair to force students to take those pre-graduate classes?

W: I actually agree with the policy.

M: You do?

W: Yeah. Most of the honors students I know plan to attend graduate school anyway. Why not take these pre-graduate classes? I bet they'll be helpful.

M: But are they really necessary?

W: I think so. They sound like a great way to prepare students to excel in graduate school. Many students I know are worried about it. They heard it's hard because students entering into graduate school usually don't know what to expect.

M: I see your point.

W: And many never finish because they weren't prepared for graduate work.

M: Yeah, it'll be good for these students to start preparing for graduate school now.

W: Exactly. Besides, I think these classes will look really good on a graduate school application. Those people I know who have taken pre-graduate classes almost always get accepted into graduate school.

M: Wow, that's great. Especially considering how competitive our English graduate program is.

▸ Step 3 - Sample Response

The announcement says that it is now mandatory for English students planning to attend graduate school to take pre-graduate courses. The woman agrees with this idea. She says that the classes are a good way to help students succeed in graduate school by preparing them early on. She supports this point by saying that many graduate students drop out because they are not prepared for graduate level work. She thinks the new pre-graduate classes will help them to know what to expect. Also, she believes that they will give students an advantage on their graduate school applications. She says that everyone she knows who has taken pre-graduate courses has been accepted into graduate school.

Q3 Practice 2

▸ Step 1 - Conversation

M: Did you hear the bulletin about the new office hours for the business school counselors?

W: Yeah. I suppose that's good news.

M: It's great news. It takes forever to get an appointment with a counselor. I always have to make counseling appointments weeks in advance. It's so exasperating! Now all I have to do is walk right in.

W: But are there going to be enough counselors to handle all the students coming in? They've had problems in the past.

M: It'll be fine. See, now, all the counselors will be available at once during these three times. Before they had to be available for the whole week. And not all counselors work every day.

W: I guess so.

M: Plus, most of us have issues that only take a few minutes to solve. I never have questions that last more than two minutes. So I bet they'll be able to handle a lot of students in three days.

W: Probably. So now when you have a question, you can just show up during office hours.

M: Precisely. It's going to make my life much easier.

▸ Step 3 - Sample Response

The announcement says that business counselors will now be holding open office hours to answer student questions. The man thinks this is a great idea because he often has trouble getting in to see a counselor. He usually has to wait weeks for an appointment. He also thinks this new policy will solve the problem of counselor availability. Most counselors do not work every day during the week. Therefore, they are not always accessible each day. Now, according to the man, since they only need to be available for three days, all counselors should be available at once. Since most students only have questions that take a few minutes to answer, he feels like these three days will be enough to handle all the students.

Q4 Practice 1

▸ Step 1 - Lecture

W: Although it once wasn't thought possible, neuroscientists now believe that there are at least two different ways that a damaged adult brain can achieve some amount of recovery.

First, in certain areas of our brain . . . cells that have been lost through damage can be replaced by new ones. In a 1998 study of dead human brain tissue, researchers discovered that neurons, or brain cells, can actually re-grow themselves after they had suffered damage. Neurons that have not been damaged can divide into multiple neurons. This ability to regenerate can occur throughout our lives, allowing areas of the adult brain to recover to a certain degree after serious brain damage. Unfortunately, this ability can only occur in two areas of the brain.

The adult brain also has the unique ability to reorganize itself so that other parts assume the tasks of the damaged area. Take adults who have suffered from strokes, for instance . . . when the brain is damaged by a stroke, patients often lose such functions as motor control, memory, or the ability to speak and understand language. However, researchers have found that often what happens after a stroke is that uninjured—or healthy—areas of the brain will reorganize themselves to perform the same—or nearly the same—functions of the damaged areas.

▸ Step 3 - Sample Response

According to the reading, an adult brain has two ways to recover from brain damage. The professor explains that the first way is by brain cell re-growth. She says that sometimes an adult brain can re-grow cells that were lost through damage. She says that this can happen when undamaged brain cells divide to form new cells. She then explains the second way the adult brain can recover from brain damage—by reorganizing itself. The professor gives the example of those who have suffered from strokes. Sometimes when patients lose certain functions due to a stroke, the healthy parts of their brains are able to change. They can take over those functions that were found in the damaged parts of the brain.

Q4 Practice 2

▸ Step 1 - Lecture

M: Probably the most obvious downside of interactive television is that, like all television, it can influence a child's intelligence in a bad way. A recent study showed that children who are exposed to television at a young age score lower on intelligence tests than do other children, leading a pediatrics institution to conclude that children under age two should not be watching television as it could harm them cognitively. Despite this fact, interactive television systems are being made for children as young as toddlers. Studies have now estimated that children as young as a year old are watching over two hours of television a day. So interactive television simply increases the time our children spend in front of the TV, thus harming them in the long run.

Interactive television will also allow advertisers to target children in new ways. For instance, certain interactive Internet games have already been developed which advertise products to children as they're playing the games. Products like cereal, chocolate chip cookies, and beverages have all been advertised through interactive games that children can play. This is a problem because children are inherently vulnerable to advertising. They usually accept what they see or hear as fact. With interactive television, because it often works through an Internet connection, advertisers can target children based on what they learn about them—their gender, age, even their behaviors and preferences.

▸ Step 3 - Sample Response

According to the reading, interactive television can negatively affect children's intelligence and allow companies to target children. The professor expands on this first point by saying that television has been shown to be harmful for children under the age of two to watch. Tests have shown that it can lower intelligence levels. Yet there are many interactive television programs out there made especially for children under two. He also says that interactive television allows advertisers to target young children. They can sell specific products to children based on what they learn about them through the Internet. Children are easily persuaded by these advertisements and accept what they see or hear as being true.

Chapter 6 Test Questions 5 and 6

Q5 Practice 1

▸ Step 1 - Conversation

W: Hi, Brandon. How's that lab report coming along?

M: All right, I guess. I've got all the data. There's just one problem. I have no idea how to organize it all. It's really frustrating.

W: Have you talked with your professor? I bet she would have some suggestions.

M: I'm sure she would. My problem is that I have class during her office hours. I can't just go talk with her about it. And the project is due in a few days.

W: Yeah, that doesn't give you a lot of time to speak with her. Couldn't you meet with her another time when you don't have class? I'm sure she could accommodate you by making an appointment.

M: Hmm . . . I suppose I could ask her to schedule an appointment outside of office hours. But I'm afraid she might be too occupied with other classes. I'm also extremely busy.

W: Well, you might be able to work something out. Or you could just email her your questions.

M: True. That'd be a lot easier.

W: But it might be hard to clarify what you're having trouble with through email.

M: Yeah, and I'd like to be able to show her my data. It's all in my field notebook. I haven't entered it in the computer yet. Like I said, I'm not sure of the best way to organize it.

W: Well, I hope you get help somehow. I know you've put a lot of work into this lab.

▸ Step 3 - Sample Response

The man wants to ask his professor questions about his lab report. However, he has class during the professor's office hours. The woman suggests that he either make an appointment to talk with the professor another time or email the professor his questions. I think he should schedule an appointment with his professor outside of office hours. His professor is probably aware that her students may have class during her regular office hours. I am sure she would be willing to accommodate those students. Also, by meeting with his professor in person rather than through email, the man can fully explain what he is having trouble with. He will be able to work directly with his professor to come up with possible solutions.

Q5 Practice 2

▸ Step 1 - Conversation

M: So, did you decide to enroll in that creative writing course after all?

W: I still haven't decided. I'd really like to, but it's only on Tuesdays from 7 to 10 p.m. And I'm afraid to walk back to my car so late at night.

M: Yeah, I know what you mean. I get uneasy walking around campus at night sometimes, too. You know, you can always call campus security and ask for an escort.

W: I thought of that, but don't you have to pay?

M: No, not at all. It's a free service for students.

W: Really? Well, that's good to know. Still, though, I think I'd feel kinda awkward having a security guard walk me to my car. He'd have to do it once a week.

M: Yeah, I understand. You wouldn't know the person. Plus, it might be inconvenient to request a security escort once a week.

W: That's true. It'd be nice if I had a friend in the class.

M: You could always go to the class the first week and see if you know anyone. Maybe someone is walking the same way back as you are.

W: Yeah, I could do that. There could be several people in the class who also park in the student lot.

M: Then again, you might not see anyone you know. There's still the chance you might have to walk back to your car alone.

W: You're right. I'll have to think about it.

▸ Step 3 - Sample Response

The woman wants to take a creative writing class. However, it is at night, and she does not want to walk alone back to her car. The man suggests that she either ask for a security escort to walk her back to her car or find someone in class to walk with her to the student parking lot. I think she should call campus security and arrange for an escort to walk her to her car after class each week. That way, she will not have to risk walking alone if no one in her class is walking back to the student parking lot. Also, it is important that she have someone to walk with who knows how to handle dangerous situations and who can protect her.

Q6 Practice 1

▸ Step 1 - Lecture

W: Today, we enjoy tales where an unexpected person becomes the hero of the story . . . but this isn't true of Classical literature. Classicism is the period of Western literature that started during the time of the ancient Greeks and continued until about 1800 BCE. All Western literature written during this time has one characteristic in common: the heroes of the tale are never common or unexpected like today's heroes, but are always noble and of aristocratic birth. This is known as the aristocratic hero. We see the aristocratic hero portrayed again and again in Classical literature.

Perhaps one of the first and foremost examples of the aristocratic hero in Western literature is Odysseus from Homer's *The Odyssey*. Odysseus is the perfect example of the aristocratic hero. He's a legendary Greek king who spends ten years trying to get back home to reclaim his throne. We can clearly see that despite the trials Odysseus undergoes, his noble nature is never questioned. In fact, Odysseus is favored by the Greek gods, and the gods of Greek literature hardly ever favor anyone that is not of noble birth. Only aristocratic people like Odysseus could become great Greek heroes.

Twenty-four centuries and several cultures later, we see the exact same type of aristocratic hero written about in plays by William Shakespeare. The heroes of the plays that Shakespeare wrote about include people like Julius Caesar and the English kings Richard III and Henry VI, but rarely is the main hero ever of common birth. What I'm trying to say here is that even though the views of the world had changed drastically since Greek times, the view of the literary hero remained the same: he had to be of noble birth. Even the heroes of Shakespeare's light comedies were members of England's high society.

▸ Step 3 - Sample Response

The professor says that all Western Classical literature has people of noble birth as its heroes. This is known as the aristocratic hero. The professor says this idea of the aristocratic hero lasted for the entire classical era. She mentions the Greek hero Odysseus as the first example of the aristocratic hero. He is a legendary king that is favored by the gods. The professor mentions that the Greek gods rarely favor characters that are not noble. The professor then says that this characteristic of the aristocratic hero persisted for thousands of years. She mentions Shakespeare, who lived twenty-four centuries later, but who still focused largely on noble people as his heroes. Even the characters of Shakespeare's comedies were from England's high society.

Q6 Practice 2

▸ Step 1 - Lecture

M: There are several theories as to why certain ancient cities became prosperous, but one factor that cannot be disputed is the importance of water. The success of ancient cities depended on their water sources, and for this reason, many of the greatest ancient cities that we know of were located near prominent sources of water. Think about the great civilizations of Greece and Rome, both settled along the Mediterranean Sea. Historians suggest that water contributed to the success of ancient cities in two ways.

First off, water allowed certain cities to flourish because of its agricultural use. Having close access to fresh water allowed societies to grow their own food. The Sumerians, one of the earliest known civilizations, were able to settle down and form cities because they built irrigation ditches that transported water from the Tigris and Euphrates rivers to their crop fields. Living near a source of water, therefore, made agriculture possible. And having an agricultural system meant that the Sumerians didn't have to travel long distances to hunt and forage for food, giving them more time to develop arts and culture. It was their close proximity to water that allowed many of these ancient cities to thrive.

Living near water also allowed ancient peoples to develop trade. This was a critical component of civilizations like Greece and Rome because this trade made these cities prosperous. The Ancient Egyptians, for example, used the Nile River to carry valuable cargo, or material goods, from one end of their empire to the other. Eventually, extensive trade networks developed along such water highways and were used to import and export goods between civilizations. In order to participate in and prosper from this trade, it was therefore incredibly important for ancient peoples to build their cities along water routes.

▸ Step 3 - Sample Response

The professor says that the success of ancient cities depended largely on their location near large water sources. First, building ancient cities near water sources made them successful because water gave people a way to grow food. For example, the Sumerians watered their crops with water from nearby rivers. Because they did not have to search for food, they could devote more time to other things, like developing their culture. Living close to water also allowed ancient peoples to trade with each other. This made many of them prosperous. The Egyptians, for example, used the Nile River to transport goods between cities in their empire. Therefore, it was important for ancient people to build their cities along these waterways in order to trade with other civilizations.

Part 3

Chapter 7 Pronunciation

Stress on content words

▸ Step 1

1. However, I would definitely like to go to the park on my new scooter.
2. After this annual seminar is over, please do not forget to sign up for the one next year.
3. The small child was uncertain as to whether or not he should raise his hand.
4. I think it is better to keep a calendar in order to remember important dates.
5. My grandparents significantly influenced my happiness as a child.
6. Although I would like to take Saturday off, I believe it is more important that I go to the tutoring session.
7. So far, my experiences with skydiving have been fun and exciting.
8. The professor must conduct lots of research in order to publish his findings.

▸ Step 2

Even though some may think that fictional books are pointless, I believe that fictional books are a necessity for many people. First of all, fictional books can be used as teaching tools. For example, a lot of the fictional books I have read involve characters who learn important life lessons. I can apply the lessons these characters learn to my own life. Also, fictional books provide us with a necessary means of escape. Sometimes we require a period away from reality. I feel that fictional books give us just the break we need to allow us to recover from life's difficulties.

Stress on function words

▸ Step 1

1. However, Roger should know how to wash his own clothes.
2. Actually, I did guess many of the correct answers on yesterday's test.
3. Fifty years ago, my grandparents were married in Hawaii.
4. I am ready to register for my classes next week.
5. Despite evidence to the contrary, George is certain that he will get picked for the part.
6. He is not the one with the cold. I am.
7. I could participate in the game, but I really don't want to play.
8. Should you decide to attend the seminar, you will need to present a report.

▸ Step 2

1. I know you think I cannot do it, but I really can handle an after-school job.
2. Last year, it both rained and snowed during the month of June.
3. Are you absolutely certain that you cannot make the meeting today?
4. She prefers cleaning her bedroom over cleaning her bathroom.
5. I have so much homework that I do not know where to start.
6. It is impossible to trust anything that my best friend says.
7. Marketing 413 is only for business majors.
8. The instructor taught the girl to play the piano beautifully.

Chapter 8 Stress and Intonation

Changing pitch for emphasis

▸ Step 1

1. It is a bad idea to wait until the night before a test to begin studying.
2. Teenagers should have certain restrictions on their driver's licenses.
3. Are you sure you do not want to have lunch with me?
4. That is a really large piece of cake.

▸ Step 2

1. The recreational center will offer a new self-defense course. It will teach young people how to protect themselves.
2. Butterflies are usually active during the day. Moths are more active at night.
3. I prefer not to have homework over the weekends. However, I do not mind having a little bit of homework then.
4. Everyone wants to buy a beautiful house. For this reason, houses that are ugly do not sell very well.
5. The fifth-grader was a very messy worker. Her partner was very organized.
6. The woman bought a new bag at the mall downtown. It had just opened a couple of weeks before.

Commas and series with *and* or *or*

▸ Step 1

1. The man's chores included walking the dog, doing the laundry, cleaning the bathroom, and washing the car.
2. Recycling campaigns have been very successful in our city, partially due to the friendly publicity from local newspapers.
3. I was not certain whether the text should be placed at the top of the page or in the middle.
4. Young people often experience pressure from outside influences to conform to certain trends, particularly when they get into high school.
5. He could have told his mother that he had spent the evening studying, but it would not have been the truth.
6. The man was not sure whether to pick the striped tie, the green tie, or the purple tie.

Chapter 9 Pausing

▸ Step 1

1. Although the Greeks were credited with the first Western democracy, neither women nor slaves had the right to vote.
2. During the debate, the woman proved that Jason's argument was flawed, thereby embarrassing him in front of everyone.
3. Those pineapples were, in my opinion, the best fruit that I had ever tasted.
4. Many critics believe that modern movies lack what early movies possessed, namely, a strong plot and good actors.
5. Common pets in American households include birds, cats, and dogs.
6. Nevertheless, I still do not agree that animal testing is worthwhile.

▸ Step 2

1. His ability to track creatures across long distances enabled the man to compete in an annual competition where contestants tracked certain animals.
2. Many scientists contend that the universe started with a big bang, releasing enormous amounts of energy to create the solar systems and planets.
3. In the last three years, Joe's friends not only supported him during his illness, but they did everything in their power to make life easier for him so that he could recover more quickly.
4. Neela, a foreign exchange student from India, came from a small village in the mountains that depended almost entirely on farming.

Pause and pitch

▸ Step 1

1. Remember that when the timer rings, it is time to give the baby his bottle.
2. Ultimately, a person's success in life depends on two things: hard work and dedication.
3. Albert Einstein, the scientist known for his strange hair, came up with his theory of relativity in 1915.
4. A college education should be provided for by the government, according to my economics teacher, Ms. Brown.
5. Since she had disobeyed her parents earlier, Emily was forbidden to leave her room for the rest of the night.

6. On the other hand, I do not believe that art should replace reading, writing, and arithmetic as a student's main priorities in school.

Practice Test 1

Question 3

M: Hey, Jane. What's going on?

W: Well, I saw an announcement in the paper today about Green Acres being shut down. I'm pretty disappointed.

M: Me, too. I liked that restaurant. Why are they closing it down?

W: They said that it wasn't popular with students, but that's probably because they didn't advertise the restaurant anywhere. I remember seeing exactly two advertisements around campus during the three months that it has been open for business.

M: You're right. I didn't know it was there for a long time.

W: They're also saying that the cost of the food is too high. It doesn't really seem fair. Obviously, the food is going to cost more because it's healthier for you.

M: That makes sense to me.

W: I mean, I'm happy to pay an extra dollar or two for my meals if I'm confident that what I'm eating is nutritious and good for me. And I know many students that feel the same way.

M: Well, perhaps we'll get lucky and they'll reconsider their decision.

W: I hope so. There's no other healthy restaurant like it here on campus.

Question 4

W: The vaccination against smallpox is one of the most successful ways vaccines have been used. About 200 years ago, smallpox was a common and deadly disease—if you contracted smallpox, there was a twenty to thirty percent chance that you would die. Yet when doctors introduced a vaccine for smallpox in 1796, it helped the body to develop a crucial resistance against the disease. This resistance occurred through two stages.
Initially, the body developed antibodies, or special cells, to destroy the disease. In order to develop these antibodies, a weakened form of smallpox had to be administered to the patient through a vaccine. Then the patient's immune system could recognize the disease. The weakened smallpox disease was not strong enough to kill the patient, but it was enough to cause the body to generate antibodies—specially designed cells to fight against smallpox. These antibodies were released into the patient's bloodstream and attacked the weakened smallpox disease, destroying it in the process.
After the first stage, the patient's body then stored some of these smallpox antibodies in case of a future smallpox infection. If the patient encountered the more lethal smallpox disease in the future, the patient had the antibodies ready to destroy the disease shortly after infection. In this way, the smallpox vaccine eradicated the disease. Today the smallpox disease has been killed off completely.

Question 5

M: Hi, Belinda. How are things going?

W: Not so good. I'm really tired.

M: You look tired. What's the problem?

W: Well, things with my roommate Samantha are getting worse.

M: What do you mean?

W: Remember how she was talking on her cell phone really late at night?

M: Yeah. I thought you had asked her to stop.

W: I did. She stopped for a while, but she's started doing it again. I haven't been sleeping well all of this week because of it.

M: Well, why don't you go talk to the resident advisor for your dorm room floor?

W: Well, I thought about that. The problem is, our R.A. is really strict. And Samantha has already gotten in trouble before with the R.A.

M: Really? What about?

W: Samantha's former roommate reported her to the same R.A. last year. I'm afraid that if I report Samantha again to the R.A., then Samantha will get in trouble.

M: I see your point. Although I do think that Samantha deserves to get in trouble for not stopping her behavior after she's been asked. Still, I understand that she's your friend.

W: Yes, she is. I just don't know what to do. I've got to get some sleep.

M: Have you thought about just switching rooms, then?

W: Yeah, but I'm not thrilled with the idea of having to pack up all my stuff.
M: It might be a lot of trouble. But if it means you get a good night's sleep, it could be worth it.
W: Maybe you're right. Thanks for the advice.

Question 6

M: Today we're going to discuss language divergence —how one language can diverge into multiple languages. It's generally believed by linguists that all the languages of today originated from a common proto-language thousands of years ago. A proto-language is the ancestor of modern languages. Now, as time passed and people began to split into different tribes, this original proto-language began to evolve independently in each tribe. The process of language divergence has begun. When a language begins to diverge like this, it usually goes through two key stages: first, it separates into multiple dialects, and eventually these dialects become two or more separate languages.
Dialects occur when one language begins to be altered into two or more versions. This may occur when people of one language adapt existing words to talk about new concepts. These alterations in language form what are known as dialects, different variations of the same language. Now, dialects are not yet separate, different languages. They're simply different versions of one language. For example, compare the speech of people in the United Kingdom to the speech of Americans. They're speaking the same language—English—but differently. Although they pronounce words differently and use different terminology, they are speaking different dialects of English.
Eventually, as time elapses, dialects can become so dissimilar from one another that they become their own individual language. French and Spanish are good illustrations of this. Each of these languages is different from the other. A Spanish person would not generally understand a French person without knowing the other's language. However, if you look attentively at both languages, you'll find that they do have many similarities. This is evidence that Spanish and French both evolved from one common language: a proto-language. Therefore, we can say that French and Spanish originated from the same language.

Practice Test 2

Question 3

W: Hi, Wallace. How's it going?
M: Not so great since they announced that the publications class was cancelled.
W: Oh yeah, I heard about that—were you planning on taking it?
M: Yes, I was. It was the last class I needed to graduate.
W: I'm really sorry.
M: Yeah. I mean, I realize that Professor Thomson is on extended leave, but I know of another person that could easily teach it.
W: Oh really? Another professor?
M: No. Actually, it's a former student of Professor Thomson's who took the publications class last year. She's a graduate student now, but I know she'd make a great student teacher.
W: Does she know a lot about publishing?
M: She probably knows more about publishing than most of the professors.
W: Didn't they say that not enough students were interested in the class, too?
M: Yes, that was the official announcement from the committee, but I know of at least ten other students besides myself that were planning on taking that publications class.
W: That is upsetting . . . I can understand why you're angry.
M: Well, I'm hoping that if I talk to the right people, I can convince them to reverse their decision.

Question 4

W: There are actually a couple of physiological differences which allow male songbirds to produce more complex songs than those of female songbirds.
First, there's a difference in the song-producing parts of songbird brains. It all comes down to a part called the robustus archisriatalis, or RA. This is an area of the brain responsible for song production in birds. As it turns out, the size of the RA in male songbirds is significantly larger than those in female songbirds. In zebra finches, the RA is at least five times larger in males than in females. So male birds simply have a better ability to produce songs because they have bigger song-producing mechanisms.

There's also a difference in the amount of a hormone, or chemical substance, found in the brains of male and female songbirds. This hormone is produced outside of the brain in many species. However, the male songbird's brain is able to produce this hormone on its own. In past studies, portions of male songbirds' brains were observed to produce this hormone. Hence, male songbirds have more of this hormone present in the brain, accounting for their more elaborate songs. And just to show that these hormones play a major part in birdsong, experiments have revealed that when this hormone is inserted under the skin of baby female songbirds, they too develop more elaborate songs.

Question 5

M: Hey, Jill, you look stressed out—what's going on?

W: Oh . . . hey. Yeah, I'm stressed. There's a big group project coming up next week in one of my classes. I'm expected to speak in front of a room full of other students.

M: Oh, that's right. You hate speaking in front of crowds.

W: Yeah, it makes me really nervous. I always do badly.

M: Well, is there any way that your group could do all the presenting for you? I mean, you could do most of the research and writing for the project. Then you would've done a fair share of the work, and could just let other members of your group do the speaking.

W: Well, I've considered it. I'm pretty sure that the professor would notice, though. It could hurt my grade, even if I did a lot of the research.

M: Yeah, you don't want to hurt your grade, that's for sure. How about you just do a lot of preparation for the speaking?

W: What do you mean?

M: Well, get your speaking portion ready far in advance. Then just practice it a lot until it's basically second nature to you. That way, you'll know it by heart and won't have to worry about messing up.

W: It's a good idea, but I've done that in the past and it just hasn't worked. I still get really nervous and mess up.

M: Well, I don't know what else to suggest. I hope you can figure it out. Good luck, Jill.

W: Thanks for the recommendations. I'll let you know how it goes.

Question 6

M: On our planet, we have a small quantity of plants that are carnivorous—rather than getting all their energy from sunlight, these plants actually consume insects. Carnivorous plants have evolved unique methods of trapping insects. They then digest them and get their required nutrients from the insects' bodies. So why don't we see these types of plants growing everywhere? Scientists have a theory about this. They believe that carnivorous plants require a special kind of environment in which to thrive: carnivorous plants must inhabit areas where the soil does not have many nutrients, and they must inhabit places with lots of moisture.

OK, first, carnivorous plants seem only to flourish in environments like swamps, where the soil quality is very poor. Oftentimes carnivorous plants that are cultivated by humans die, and scientists believe this is because they are usually given too many nutrients. Now, most plants require lots of nutrients in the soil to grow. However, carnivorous plants appear to be exactly opposite because they get their nutrients from the insects they catch, so they don't need lots of nutrients from the soil. Carnivorous plants seem to compensate for a lack of soil nutrients by getting their nutrients from their prey.

In addition, these plants need a lot of moisture in the air—they grow best in areas with high humidity: this makes sense when you think about the environments where these carnivorous plants evolved. Scientists have also observed that carnivorous plants that are allowed to dry out often die (although there are some exceptions to this rule). In fact, many of these plants require moisture in order to trap insects. For example, the pitcher plant uses moisture to drown its insect prey. So generally, carnivorous plants need a great deal of moisture if they're going to grow well.

Answer Key

Part 1

Chapter 1 Organizing Speech

Q1 Practice 1

▸ Step 1

Possible Related Ideas and Expressions:
city: village, urban center, downtown
visit: travel, tour, go to
fascinating: amazing, interesting, appealing
enjoy: like, value, favor

▸ Step 2

Useful Expressions:
family originated, always wanted to see, able to witness, history, buildings and places, captivated, exploring

Q1 Practice 2

▸ Step 1

Possible Related Ideas and Expressions:
type: style, form, variety
job: work, employment, trade
choose: select, want, go for
enable: let, permit, be able to

▸ Step 2

Useful Expressions:
prefer this job because, have always been fascinated by, would allow me to, enable me to, would get to, observe, experiences, exciting

Q1 Practice 3

▸ Step 1

Possible Related Ideas and Expressions:
bad: terrible, unpleasant, nasty
situation: event, incident, experience
important: chief, significant, major
lesson: example, teaching, education

▸ Step 2

Useful Expressions:
more important than, wanted, even though, finally, some goals are not worth the risk

Q2 Practice 1

▸ Step 1

Possible Related Ideas and Expressions:
prefer: want, wish, choose
live: exist, inhabit, reside
mountain: height, pile, hill
water sports: surfing, swimming, scuba diving

▸ Step 2

Opinion 1
Useful Expressions:
prefer, hikes and backpacking, enjoy going, very rewarding, able to, favorite sports

Opinion 2
Useful Expressions:
prefer, learn how to, lifelong dream, have always wanted, very peaceful, not ever have to endure, want to stay

Q2 Practice 2

▸ Step 1

Possible Related Ideas and Expressions:
friends: pals, buddies, companions
relationship: connection, bond, union
difficult: hard, tough, demanding
support: assist, cheer on, defend

▸ Step 2

Opinion 1
Useful Expressions:
prefer to have, build strong relationships, in my experience, can be overwhelming, hard to divide my time, have time for myself

Opinion 2
Useful Expressions:
prefer to have, get to know lots of people, someone to talk to, more support, feel isolated, better able to, experience many different things

Q2 Practice 3

▸ Step 1

Possible Related Ideas and Expressions:
money: riches, wealth, currency
summer vacation: break, rest, relaxation
busy: hard-working, active, industrious
boring: dull, dreary, unexciting

▸ **Step 2**

Opinion 1
Useful Expressions:
spending money, go on trips, remarkable experience, could not have afforded it, often get bored, rather keep busy

Opinion 2
Useful Expressions:
time to rest, worked so hard, did not get enough sleep, recuperate, time to do things, rather hang out with friends

Chapter 2 Synthesizing Information

Q3 Practice 1

▸ **Step 1**

Suggested Keywords/Key Phrases:
computer lab, printing paper, waste, money saved, computers

Sample Restatement:
The university computer lab will no longer provide printing paper for students. Students must use their own paper to print materials. This is because students have been wasting the university's printing paper. The money the university saves will be spent on purchasing more computers.

▸ **Step 2**

Suggested Keywords/Key Phrases:
distressing, school-related, more computers, lower student demand, lab fee

Sample Restatement:
The man and woman are distressed to hear about the university's decision. The woman remarks that she always prints out materials in the lab that are school-related. The man then comments that the money the university saves will be used to buy more computers. However, the woman thinks that there will be a lower student demand for the computer lab. Since students will no longer want to use the lab, they will not want to pay the lab fees. This means less money for the school.

▸ **Step 3**

Opinion: The woman disagrees with the university's decision.

Reason 1: She believes the university is wrong to say that students use the printing paper to print materials unrelated to school.

Detail: Everyone she knows, including herself, prints scholarly materials.

Reason 2: The school will lose money from lab fees, which means less money for new computers.

Detail: She believes student demand for the computer lab will go down if they have to bring their own paper, and students will not want to pay lab fees if they do not use the lab.

▸ **Step 4**

Useful Expressions:
students must use own paper, disagrees with decision, students print scholarly material, fewer students will pay lab fee, less money for new computers

Q3 Practice 2

▸ **Step 1**

Suggested Keywords/Key Phrases:
April 15, parking tickets, discourage student parking, emergency vehicles, closer parking lot

Sample Restatement:
On April 15, the price of parking tickets will be raised to discourage students from parking along the street. Parking along the street makes it harder for emergency vehicles to get to fire lanes. We also hope to use the money raised by the increase in parking tickets to build a parking lot closer to campus.

▸ **Step 2**

Suggested Keywords/Key Phrases:
$35-$50, customers, bad for business, half hour walk, current parking lot

Sample Restatement:
The man agrees with the rise in parking tickets from $35 to $50. He mentions that when students park on the street, they prevent customers from parking in front of the shops. He believes this is bad for businesses. He is also hoping that the money from parking tickets can be used to create a parking lot closer to campus. The current parking lot is too far away, and it takes the man a half hour to walk to class from there.

▸ **Step 3**

Opinion: The man believes that the rise in parking tickets is a good idea.

Reason 1: It will keep students from illegally parking along the street.

Detail: This will allow customers to park there, which will mean better business for the shops along the street.

Reason 2: The money can be used to build a parking lot closer to campus.

Detail: It takes the man a half hour to walk to class from the current parking lots.

▸ **Step 4**

Useful Expressions:
increase in cost of parking tickets, agrees with decision, students hurt businesses, customers cannot park, lot is too far away, less time walking to class

Q3 Practice 3

▸ **Step 1**

Suggested Keywords/Key Phrases:

paper course catalogues, online course catalogues, register, paper and ink, convenient

Sample Restatement:

The university will be switching from paper course catalogues to online course catalogues. From now on, students will register for classes through the online catalogue. This will save the university the costs of paper and ink. It will also make it more convenient for students to register for classes.

▸ **Step 2**

Suggested Keywords/Key Phrases:

other ways to raise money, inconvenient, sign up, challenge, registrar

Sample Restatement:

The man disagrees with the university's decision to switch from paper course catalogues to online course catalogues. He thinks there are other ways for the university to save money. The woman points out that It will be easier for students to sign up for classes now, but the man disagrees. He thinks using the online course catalogue will be inconvenient for students. It will be a challenge to learn how to use it. He thinks the registrar will be visited by lots of students who are having problems with the new system.

▸ **Step 3**

Opinion: The man disagrees with the university's decision to switch from paper course catalogues to online course catalogues.

Reason 1: He thinks there are other ways for the university to save money.

Detail: The university can save money by sending emails rather than posting announcements.

Reason 2: He feels that the online catalogue will be more inconvenient for students who are registering.

Detail: Students will have to learn how to navigate through a new system.

▸ **Step 4**

Useful Expressions:

paper catalogue replaced online, disagrees with decision, can save money in other ways, inconvenient, students will visit registrar anyway

Q4 Practice 1

▸ **Step 1**

Suggested Keywords/Key Phrases:

universal, warm colors, warmth and comfort, cool colors, confidence

Sample Restatement:

Colors are connected with certain emotions and can be used to affect emotions in a universal way. Colors are separated into two categories based on emotion. Warm colors are colors like red. They make people feel warmth and comfort. Cool colors are colors like blue. They make people feel more confident.

▸ **Step 2**

Suggested Keywords/Key Phrases:

pink, opponent's locker rooms, loss of energy, blue, job interviews

Sample Restatement:

The professor describes how colors can influence people. Warm colors like pink make people feel comfortable. For this reason, some sports teams paint their opponent's locker rooms pink to get them to lose energy. Since cool colors like blue are connected with confidence, those applying for jobs are often told to wear blue to display confidence during interviews.

▸ **Step 3**

Warm colors: colors like red and pink, associated with warmth and comfort

Example of how they are used: many sports teams paint their opponents' locker rooms pink, hoping it will cause opponents to lose energy

Cool colors: colors like blue and purple, associated with calmness and confidence

Example of how they are used: people often encouraged to wear blue to portray confidence at job interviews

▸ **Step 4**

Useful Expressions:
warm colors create warmth, cool colors inspire confidence, team paints opponents' locker room pink, comforting so opposing team loses energy, wear blue to interview, seem confident

Q4 Practice 2

▸ **Step 1**

Suggested Keywords/Key Phrases:
social structure, resources, order, conflicts, survival

Sample Restatement:
A dominance hierarchy is a social structure among certain species of animals. It consists of a dominant animal that controls how resources are used. The dominant animal keeps order within the dominance hierarchy. It also solves conflicts between other animals. Dominance hierarchies are necessary for the survival of some species.

▸ **Step 2**

Suggested Keywords/Key Phrases:
rank, baboon, highly structured, scarce resources, savanna

Sample Restatement:
The professor says that baboons use a highly-structured dominance hierarchy. She mentions that baboons use ranks to keep order in baboon groups. They are ruled by a dominant leader. The professor also says that dominance hierarchies help baboons avoid disputes over scarce resources. This is more important for savanna baboons because they live in a place where food is rarer.

▸ **Step 3**

Species that uses dominance hierarchies: baboons

Point 1: used to maintain order

Example: formed through a ranking system with a dominant leader in charge

Point 2: used to manage disputes over scarce resources

Example: Savanna baboons have stricter dominance hierarchies than forest baboons do because food on the savanna is scarce.

▸ **Step 4**

Useful Expressions:
dominance hierarchies maintain order, resolve conflicts, baboons use ranking system, leader must manage resources and aggression

Q4 Practice 3

▸ **Step 1**

Suggested Keywords/Key Phrases:

continental drift, Alfred Wegener, Pangea, fossils, rock formations

Sample Restatement:

Alfred Wegener believed that at one time, the Earth only had one big continent called Pangea. However, the large continent eventually broke up. The pieces moved away from each other in what Wegener called continental drift. Yet evidence of Pangea can be found through similar fossils and rock formations found across today's continents.

▸ **Step 2**

Suggested Keywords/Key Phrases:

fit, Africa and South America, additional evidence, marine reptile fossil, sandstone hills

Sample Restatement:

Wegener first noticed that the coasts of Africa and South America seemed to fit together, suggesting continental drift. Additional evidence to support Wegener's hypothesis was found in fossil records and rock formations. Fossil records of an ancient marine reptile are found in both Africa and South America. Also, there are similar sandstone hills on both the coasts of Africa and South America.

▸ **Step 3**

Continental drift: continents were once one landmass, broke up and drifted away from each other, forming today's continents

Evidence 1: similar fossils found on different continents

Example: fossils of ancient marine reptile found in both Africa and South America

Evidence 2: similar rock formations found on different continents

Example: same type of sandstone hills on west coast of South America is found on east coast of Africa

▸ **Step 4**

Useful expressions:
continental drift, continents were one landmass, fossils and rock formations, ancient marine reptile, similar coasts and minerals

Chapter 3 Stating Opinions and Summarizing

Q5 Practice 1

▸ **Step 1**

Problem: The woman is getting a C in her organic chemistry class and needs a B average to keep her scholarship.

Solution 1: Request to take the class as a pass or fail

Solution 2: Attend tutoring sessions for help

▸ **Step 2**

Opinion 1

Problem: The woman is getting a C in organic chemistry, but she needs to have a B average to keep her scholarship.

Best solution: I think the best solution is for the woman to request to take the class as a pass or fail.

Reason 1: She is too busy to take tutoring, and it may make her fall behind in other classes.

Reason 2: A pass or fail will not affect her grade negatively.

Opinion 2

Problem: The woman is getting a C in her organic chemistry class and needs a B average to keep her scholarship.

Best solution: I think the best solution is for the woman to attend the tutoring sessions and get help for organic chemistry.

Reason 1: It would be worthwhile to study with people who can help prepare her for the tests.

Reason 2: If she does well in the class, it will not matter with a pass or fail.

▸ **Step 3**

Opinion 1
Useful expressions:
C in organic chemistry, improve grade, request pass or fail, too busy, fall behind, will not affect GPA

Opinion 2
Useful expressions:
C in organic chemistry, improve grade, tutor, learn material better, raise GPA

Q5 Practice 2

▸ **Step 1**

Problem: The man will not be back in time to go on a field trip with his class, and it is a big part of his grade.

Solution 1: Meet up with the class the next day. (Saturday)

Solution 2: Ask the professor for an alternative assignment.

▸ **Step 2**

Opinion 1

Problem: The man will not be back in time to go on a field trip with his class, and it is a big part of his grade.

Best solution: I think the best solution is to catch up with his class on Saturday morning.

Reason 1: The mountain signs will make it easy for him to find his class.

Reason 2: He will not have to worry about the professor allowing him to do an alternative assignment.

Opinion 2

Problem: The man will not be back in time to go on a field trip with his class, and it is a big part of his grade.

Best solution: I think the best solution is to ask the professor for an alternative assignment.

Reason 1: The professor should understand that the man has an emergency and should be willing to give him another assignment.

Reason 2: The man will not have to worry about getting lost on the mountain trails.

▸ **Step 3**

Opinion 1
Useful Expressions:
grandfather in hospital, field trip, meet class Saturday morning, follow signs, no alternative assignment

Opinion 2
Useful Expressions:
grandfather in hospital, field trip, alternative assignment, professor will probably allow, no risk of getting lost

Q5 Practice 3

▸ **Step 1**

Problem: The woman does not have enough money to live in the dorms.

Solution 1: Get a work-study job

Solution 2: Take out a loan

▸ **Step 2**

Opinion 1

Problem: The woman does not have enough money to live in the dorms.

Best solution: I feel that the best solution is for the woman to get a work-study job.

Reason 1: This will allow for the woman to live on campus without going into debt.

Reason 2: A work-study job will be able to work around her busy schedule.

Opinion 2

Problem: The woman does not have enough money to live in the dorms.

Best solution: I feel that the best solution is for the woman to take out a loan.

Reason 1: This will allow for the woman to live on campus without having to work, letting her concentrate more on schoolwork.

Reason 2: She will be able to pay for all her housing expenses at the beginning of the semester.

▸ **Step 3**

Opinion 1
Useful Expressions:
live on campus, cannot afford, work-study job, pay costs, no debt, work around school schedule

Opinion 2
Useful Expressions:
live on campus, cannot afford, take out loan, do not have to work, concentrate on school, less stress, pay right away

Q6 Practice 1

▸ **Step 1**

Minimalism is a movement where artists reduced artwork to its basic shapes and colors.

Design techniques used by minimalist artists:
a) simple, uniform objects in their artwork
b) lots of objects in repeating patterns

Carl Andre's "Steel Zinc Plain":
Used the technique of uniform shapes
Physical description: square-shaped plates arranged in a checkerboard pattern people can walk on

Dan Flavin's "Monument for V. Tatlin":
Used the technique of repetition

Physical description: fluorescent tubes arranged in a simple miniature tower; inspired by grand monument

▸ **Step 3**

Useful Expressions:
minimalist artists, basic colors and shapes, simple and unique, repetition, checkerboard pattern, uniform shapes, florescent tubes

Q6 Practice 2

▸ Step 1

Charisma definition: ability to inspire enthusiasm and affection in other people

Traits of charismatic leadership:
a) creates a vision that is appealing to followers
b) demonstrates this vision through action

Dr. Martin Luther King, Jr.:
He demonstrated the ability to create an appealing vision.
His accomplishments: Believing all men were created equal, he helped American government pass laws giving every Americans certain rights.

General Patton:
He demonstrated his vision through action.
He showed this by actively demonstrating how to get rid of a traffic jam.

▸ Step 3

Useful Expressions:
charismatic leadership, leaders attract followers, create an appealing vision, Dr. Martin Luther King Jr., demonstrate vision through action, General Patton

Q6 Practice 3

▸ Step 1

The Asch experiment revealed that the pressure to conform greatly influences people's decisions.

Description of Asch experiment: Asch showed students note cards with three black lines written on them and asked questions about the lines; all but the last student were instructed to give the same wrong answer.

Response of the last student: One-third of the time, the last student replied with the same wrong answer, even though it was different from what he had observed.

What Asch believed would happen: He believed that the last student would almost always resist group pressure and give the right answer.

What actually happened: Students were willing to sacrifice what they knew was true in order to conform.

▸ Step 3

Useful Expressions:
Asch experiment, pressure to conform, influences decisions, students told to give wrong answer, last student gave same answer, different than what was observed

| Vocabulary Review 1 |

1. (B) 2. (D) 3. (A)
4. (A) 5. (C) 6. (D)
7. (C) 8. (B)

9. (A) 10. (D) 11. (B)
12. (C) 13. (A) 14. (D)
15. (C)

16. afford 17. scholarship 18. ignorant
19. unscholarly 20. penalty

21. (D) 22. (E) 23. (B)
24. (A) 25. (C)

| Vocabulary Review 2 |

1. (B) 2. (C) 3. (D)
4. (B) 5. (C) 6. (D)
7. (A) 8. (C)

9. (B) 10. (D) 11. (C)
12. (B) 13. (A) 14. (B)
15. (C)

16. monument 17. traffic jam
18. grandeur 19. remarkable 20. endures

21. rebuke 22. dejection 23. varied
24. assume 25. subsequently

Part 2

Chapter 4 Test Questions 1 and 2

Q1 Practice 1

▸ Step 1

Transitions:

For instance, because, Also

Sentence Order:

(C) (E) (A) (D) (F) (B)

▸ Step 2

Suggested Answers:

1. The speaker's favorite place is the park in the downtown area of her city.
2. The speaker likes to watch people interacting with each other, and she likes playing volleyball there.
3. The speaker likes to do these activities there because she enjoys watching people and because playing volleyball allows her to make friends and take a break from schoolwork.

▸ Step 3

Helpful Expressions:

park downtown, watch people, interaction, play volleyball, meet friends, exercise, break from school

▸ Step 4

Possible Responses:

1. My favorite place to go in my city is the movie theater.
2. I like to watch new movies and eat popcorn with my friends there.
3. I like to watch movies because they are interesting and exciting and I can relax with my friends.

Q1 Practice 2

▸ Step 1

Transitions:

because, before, Even though, also, as a child

Sentence Order:

(F) (D) (A) (C) (E) (B)

▸ Step 2

Suggested Answers:

1. The speaker's favorite book was about a boy who uses his imagination to turn his room into a magical forest, where he becomes the king of all the Wild Things. The Wild Things are monsters in the forest.
2. The speaker liked this book as a child because it had lots of pictures and it was easy to memorize.
3. What was surprising about the monsters is that even though they were supposed to be scary, the pictures made them look silly and likeable.

▸ Step 3

Helpful Expressions:

Where the Wild Things Are, imagination, great pictures, silly monsters, simple story, easy to memorize

▸ Step 4

Possible Responses:

1. My favorite book was about a boy who became a wizard.
2. I liked this book because it was exciting and it had magic in it.
3. What was surprising about the book was that the boy could fly and cast magic spells.

Q1 Practice 3

▸ Step 1

Transition Words/Phrases:

before, however, also

▸ Step 2

Helpful Expressions:

positive impact, ninth-grade teacher, passion for literature, fun, deal with conflicts, follow example

▸ Step 4

Possible Answers

Teacher: High school gym teacher Mr. Goodwin
Reason 1: Before high school, I did not like to exercise.
Reason 2: However, Mr. Goodwin taught me that exercising can be fun.

Q1 Practice 4

▸ Step 1

Transition Words/Phrases:
first, plus

▸ Step 2

Helpful Expressions:
mother's advice, take schoolwork seriously, good grades, college scholarship, good study habits, eligible for jobs

▸ Step 4

Possible Answers:
Grandfather's **advice**: Honesty is always the best policy.
Reason 1: Lying hurts others.
Detail: When I was little, I broke a glass and told my parents that my sister did it. My sister was very upset.
Reason 2: It hurts me more to lie than to tell the truth.
Detail: I got into much more trouble for lying than for breaking the glass.

Q2 Practice 1

▸ Step 1

Transitions:
secondly, this way, also

Sentence Order:
(E) (D) (A) (F) (C) (B)

▸ Step 2

Suggested Answers:
1. The speaker wishes to attend a local college.
2. One reason the speaker gives for preferring a local college is that she would be closer to her family, so they would be there to help her through any difficulties.
3. The second reason the speaker gives is that she believes local colleges provide just as good an education as national universities at half the cost.

▸ Step 3

Helpful Expressions:
prefer local college, family nearby, give advice, support, good education, less cost, attain success

▸ Step 4

Possible Responses:
1. I would like to attend a national university.
2. I would like to attend a national university because I want to be independent and have new experiences.
3. I feel that a national university would offer me more opportunities for employment after I graduate.

Q2 Practice 2

▸ Step 1

Transitions:
since, also, primarily, in contrast

Sentence Order:
(E) (C) (F) (B) (D) (A)

▸ Step 2

Suggested Answers:
1. The speaker prefers to visit educational places.
2. The first reason the speaker gives for his preference is that educational places help him to understand and appreciate the area that he is visiting.
3. The speaker says that educational places like museums are distinctive to an area, whereas places solely devoted to entertainment can be found anywhere.

▸ Step 3

Helpful Expressions:
prefer educational places, curious about area and people, understand and appreciate history and culture, distinctive, will not see again

▸ Step 4

Possible Responses:
1. I would prefer to visit entertaining places when I travel.
2. I prefer entertaining places because I want to have fun when I go somewhere.
3. In my opinion, educational places are often boring and do not show what people are really like, while places for entertainment shows what people like to do.

Q2 Practice 3

▸ **Step 1**

Transition Words/Phrases:
first, also, secondly, consequently

▸ **Step 2**

Helpful Expressions:
parents should influence material, best judges, aware of struggles, helpful for curriculum, children may feel uncomfortable, can intervene

▸ **Step 4**

Possible Answers
Should parents influence curriculum? No
Reason 1: Teachers are educated to know what children should learn.
Reason 2: A curriculum is designed to help all children learn the same things at the same rate.
Reason 3: If all parents were allowed to influence a curriculum, then no one would ever agree.

Q2 Practice 4

▸ **Step 1**

Transition Words/Phrases:
also, however

▸ **Step 2**

Helpful Expressions:
not good to be constantly active, drains energy, bodies need rest, relax and recharge, counterproductive, do things more efficiently

▸ **Step 4**

Possible Answers
Is it good to be constantly active? Yes
Reason 1: Being active keeps life interesting and exciting.
Reason 2: Being active prevents laziness and procrastination.
Reason 3: Being active helps your mind and your body to stay healthy and stimulated.

Chapter 5 Test Questions 3 and 4

Q3 Practice 1

▸ **Step 1**

Main idea: Honors students planning to go to graduate school must now take pre-graduate classes.
Key points: The classes will help the transition from college to graduate school.
The classes will enhance students' graduate school applications.

Opinion: The woman agrees with the English Department's decision for mandatory pre-graduate classes.

Reason 1: Pre-graduate classes are a good way to help English majors succeed in graduate school.

Reason 2: These classes will give students an advantage on their graduate school applications.

▸ **Step 2**

Possible Sample Response:

The announcement says that English students planning to attend graduate school must now take pre-graduate courses. The woman agrees with this idea. She says that the classes will help students succeed in graduate school by preparing them early on. She supports this point by saying that many graduate students drop out because they are not prepared for graduate level work. She thinks the classes will help them know what to expect. Also, she believes they will give students an advantage on their graduate school applications. She says that everyone she knows who has taken pre-graduate courses has been accepted into graduate school.

Q3 Practice 2

▸ **Step 1**

Main idea: School counselors now have open office hours three times per week to see students.
Key points: Students can have their questions answered more quickly.
There will be enough counselors available to meet demand.

Opinion: The man thinks that the business school's decision to have open walk-in hours for counseling is a good idea.

Reason 1: He often has trouble getting in to see counselors in a timely manner.

Example: He currently needs to schedule counseling appointments weeks in advance.

Reason 2: His questions only take a few minutes to resolve.

Example: Hence, counselors should be able to see all of the students with problems.

▸ Step 2

Possible Sample Response:

The announcement says that business counselors will hold open office hours to answer students' questions. The man thinks this is a great idea. He usually has to wait weeks for an appointment with a counselor. He also thinks this new policy will solve the problem of counselor availability. Most counselors do not work every day. Therefore, they are not always accessible. Now, according to the man, counselors will be available at once. Since most questions only take a few minutes to answer, he feels that open office hours will be enough to handle all the students.

Q4 Practice 1

▸ Step 1

Main idea: Adults with severe brain damage may be able to recover brain functions.
Key points: Parts of the adult brain can sometimes create new cells.
The brain can adapt to take on new functions.

Ways the Adult Brain Can Recover from Damage

Way 1: The adult brain can re-grow cells lost through damage

How this happens: Undamaged brain cells divide to form multiple cells
How this was discovered: In a 1998 study of dead human brain tissue

Way 2: The brain can reorganize itself

How this happens: Healthy parts of the brain take over the functions of the damaged parts

Example: Stroke victims

▸ Step 2

Possible Sample Response:

According to the reading, an adult brain can recover from damage in two ways. The professor explains that the first is brain cell re-growth. She says sometimes an adult brain can re-grow cells that were lost through damage. She says this can happen when undamaged brain cells divide to form new cells. She then explains how reorganization can also help the adult brain recover from damage. The professor gives the example of stroke victims. Sometimes when patients lose certain functions due to a stroke, the healthy parts of their brains are able to change. They can take over functions that were performed by damaged parts of the brain.

Q4 Practice 2

▸ Step 1

Main idea: Interactive television has negative effects on children.
Key points: Interactive television can negatively affect children's intelligence.
Interactive television can target children for non-educational purposes.

Negative Effects of Interactive Television

Effect 1: It causes young children to watch even more television.

Study 1: Children who watch television at a young age score lower on intelligence tests than do other children.

Study 2: Children as young as a year old are watching up to two hours of television a day.

Effect 2: Interactive television allows advertisers to target children in new ways.
How this happens: Advertisers can sell specific products to children based on what they learn about them on the Internet.
Why this is a problem: Children take what they see and hear as fact.

▸ Step 2

Possible Sample Response:

According to the reading, interactive television can negatively affect children's intelligence and allow companies to target children. The professor expands on this first point by saying that television is harmful for children under the age of two to watch. Tests show that it can lower intelligence levels. Yet there are many interactive television programs made especially for children under two. He also says interactive television allows advertisers to target young children. They can sell products to children based on what they learn them through the Internet. Children are easily persuaded by these advertisements and believe what they see or hear is true.

Chapter 6 Test Questions 5 and 6

Q5 Practice 1

▸ **Step 1**

Problem: The man has some questions about a lab report that is due soon, but he has class during his professor's office hours.

Solution 1: He could make an appointment to talk to his professor another time.

Advantages: He could explain what he needs help with in detail.

Disadvantages: The professor may be too busy to see him.

Solution 2: The man could email his professor the questions.

Advantages: It would be easier than meeting with the professor.

Disadvantages: It could be hard to explain what he needs help with through email.

▸ **Step 2**

Suggested Answers:

1. The man has some questions about a lab report that is due soon, but he has class during his professor's office hours.
2. He should schedule an appointment with his professor outside of office hours.
3. I think meeting with the professor would give him the ability to explain in detail what he needs help with. Also, the professor should be willing to accommodate students who have class during her office hours.

▸ **Step 3**

Sample Response:

The man wants to talk to his professor about his lab report. However, he has class during the professor's office hours. The woman suggests he either make an appointment to talk with the professor another time or email the professor his questions. I think he should schedule an appointment outside of office hours. His professor likely knows that some students have class during her office hours. I am sure she would accommodate those students. Also, by meeting with his professor in person, the man can fully explain what he is having trouble with. He will be able to work directly with his professor to come up with solutions.

Q5 Practice 2

▸ **Step 1**

Problem: A course the student wants to take is only offered at night, and she is afraid to walk back to her car alone in the dark.

Solution 1: Request a security escort to walk her back to her car.

Advantages: The service is free, and she will always have someone well-trained to escort her to her car.

Disadvantages: It might be inconvenient and awkward to request a security escort every week.

Solution 2: Wait until class starts and then see if there is a friend in the class that would be willing to walk her back to her car.

Advantages: It would be more convenient and less awkward than requesting a security escort every week.

Disadvantages: There might not be anyone she knows taking the class.

▸ **Step 2**

Suggested Answers:

1. The woman is afraid to walk to her car at night by herself.
2. I think she should request a security escort to walk her back to her car once a week.
3. I think requesting a security escort would be better because then the girl would not have to take the chance of walking back to her car alone. Also, she will have someone with her who is well-trained to protect her.

▸ **Step 3**

Sample Response:

The woman wants to take a writing class. However, it is at night, and she does not want to walk alone back to her car. The man suggests she either ask for a security escort to her car or find someone in class to walk with her to the parking lot. I think she should ask campus security for an escort to walk her to her car. That way, she will not have to walk alone if no one in her class is walking to the student parking lot. Also, she should walk with someone who knows how to handle dangerous situations.

Q6 Practice 1

▸ Step 1

Main topic: the aristocratic hero in Western Classical literature

Shared characteristic of the aristocratic hero: noble birth

Example 1: Odysseus from Homer's *The Odyssey*

Details: Odysseus is a king of a Greek island who struggles to get home for many years; despite his trials, his noble birth is never questioned; he is favored by the gods; rarely do the gods favor anyone that is not noble.

Example 2: Heroes in the plays of William Shakespeare

Details: His characters are often kings; almost all the heroes in Shakespeare's plays are noble, even in his comedies.

▸ Step 2

Suggested Answers:

1. All Classical heroes are of noble and aristocratic birth.
2. The Greek gods typically favored those heroes who were royal.
3. The heroes of Shakespeare's plays are rarely common.

▸ Step 3

Sample Response:

The professor says that Western Classical literature has people of noble birth as its heroes. This is called the aristocratic hero. The professor says the idea of the aristocratic hero lasted for hundreds of years. She mentions the Greek hero Odysseus as one of the first aristocratic heroes. He is a legendary king favored by the gods. The professor mentions that the Greek gods rarely favor characters that are not noble. The professor then says that this characteristic of the aristocratic hero lasted for thousands of years. She mentions Shakespeare, who lived much later, but still focused largely on noble people as his heroes. Even the characters of Shakespeare's comedies were from England's high society.

Q6 Practice 2

▸ Step 1

Main topic: How water contributed to the success of ancient cities

Claim the professor makes: Success of ancient cities depended on nearby water sources

Point 1: Water sources allowed cities to develop agriculture.

Example: The ancient Sumerians, one of the first civilizations, used water from nearby rivers for crops; allowed them to settle down and develop art and culture.

Point 2: Water sources gave ancient cities the ability to trade.

Example: Ancient Egyptians used the Nile River to transport their cargo; allowed them to develop an effective trade network and become prosperous.

▸ Step 2

Suggested Answers:

1. Water sources allowed ancient cities to become great and prosperous.
2. The Sumerian civilization formed because the Sumerians used the water from rivers to develop agriculture, giving them the ability to settle down in one area.
3. The professor said that the nearby Nile River allowed Egypt to trade goods to different parts of the Empire, which allowed their cities to become prosperous.

▸ Step 3

Sample Response:

The professor says that the success of ancient cities depended largely on their location near large water sources. First, water gave people a way to grow food. For example, Sumerians watered their crops with water from nearby rivers. Because they did not have to search for food, they could devote more time to developing their culture. Living close to water also allowed ancient peoples to trade with each other. This made many of them prosperous. The Egyptians, for example, used the Nile River to transport good between cities in their empire. Therefore, it was important for ancient people to build cities along waterways in order to trade with other civilizations.

| Vocabulary Review 3 |

1. (B) 2. (A) 3. (C)
4. (D) 5. (A) 6. (C)
7. (B) 8. (A) 9. (D)
10. (B) 11. (A) 12. (C)
13. (B) 14. (B) 15. (A)

16. (B) 17. (D) 18. (B)
19. (A) 20. (D) 21. (B)
22. (B) 23. (A) 24. (C)
25. (D) 26. (A) 27. (D)
28. (C) 29. (D) 30. (C)

31. neuroscientists
32. cognitively 33. permanent
34. hard-wired 35. cells 36. regenerate
37. tissue 38. adapt 39. strokes
40. motor

41. conceal 42. mystify 43. fulfilling
44. swimming 45. sensible

46. (O) 47. (S) 48. (O)
49. (S) 50. (S)

| Vocabulary Review 4 |

1. (D) 2. (B) 3. (A)
4. (C) 5. (B) 6. (D)
7. (C) 8. (B) 9. (A)
10. (A) 11. (C) 12. (A)
13. (B) 14. (A) 15. (C)

16. (D) 17. (B) 18. (A)
19. (B) 20. (B) 21. (A)
22. (D) 23. (B) 24. (C)
25. (A) 26. (D) 27. (D)
28. (C) 29. (A) 30. (D)

31. impact 32. assistance 33. facilitate
34. transition 35. applicants 36. pool
37. park 38. campus 39. encounter
40. escort

41. out 42. off 43. up
44. down 45. back

46. (E) 47. (D) 48. (B)
49. (A) 50. (C)

Part 3

Chapter 7 Pronunciation

Stress on content words

▸ Step 1

1. However, I would definitely like to go to the park on my new scooter.
2. After this annual seminar is over, please do not forget to sign up for the one next year.
3. The small child was uncertain as to whether or not he should raise his hand.
4. I think it is better to keep a calendar in order to remember important dates.
5. My grandparents significantly influenced my happiness as a child.
6. Although I would like to take Saturday off, I believe it is more important that I go to the tutoring session.
7. So far, my experiences with skydiving have been fun and exciting.
8. The professor must conduct lots of research in order to publish his findings.

▸ Step 2

Suggested clear words in bold:

Even though some may think that fictional books are pointless, I believe that fictional books are a **necessity** for **many people**. First of all, fictional books can be used as **teaching tools**. For example, a lot of the fictional books I have read involve characters who learn **important life lessons**. I can apply the **lessons** these **characters learn** to my own life. Also, fictional books provide us with a **necessary** means of **escape**. Sometimes we require a **period** away from **reality**. I feel that fictional books give us just the break we need to allow us to recover from **life's difficulties**.

Stress on function words

▸ Step 1

1. (S) 2. (S) 3. (R)
4. (R) 5. (S) 6. (S)
7. (S), (S) 8. (R)

▸ Step 2

1. I know you **think** I cannot do it, but I really **can handle** an **after-school job**.

2. Last year, it both rained **and** snowed during the month of June.
3. Are you **absolutely** certain that you cannot make the meeting today?
4. She prefers cleaning her **bedroom** over cleaning her **bathroom**.
5. I have **so much** homework that I **do not** know where to start.
6. It is **impossible** to trust **anything** that my best friend says.
7. Marketing 413 is **only** for business majors.
8. The instructor taught the girl to play the piano **beautifully**.

Chapter 8 Stress and Intonation

Changing pitch for emphasis

▸ Step 1

1. It is a bad idea to wait until the night before a test to begin studying.
   b. It is also not wise to wait until the last minute to do homework.
2. Teenagers should have certain restrictions on their driver's licenses.
   b. However, those over 18 do not need any driving restrictions.
3. Are you sure you do not want to have lunch with me?
   b. No, I am eating lunch with another friend.
4. That is a really large piece of cake.
   b. It is way too much for me to eat.

▸ Step 2

1. The recreational center will offer a new self- defense course. It will teach young people how to protect themselves.
2. Butterflies are usually active during the day. Moths are more active at night.
3. I prefer not to have homework over the weekends. However, I do not mind having a little bit of homework then.
4. Everyone wants to buy a beautiful house. For this reason, houses that are ugly do not sell very well.
5. The fifth-grader was a very messy worker. Her partner was very organized.
6. The woman bought a new bag at the mall downtown. It had just opened a couple of weeks before.

Commas and series with *and* or *or*

▸ Step 1

1. The man's chores included walking the dog, / (↗) doing the laundry, / (↗) cleaning the bathroom, / (↗) and washing the car. (↘)
2. Recycling campaigns have been very successful in our city, / (↗) partially due to the friendly publicity from local newspapers. (↘)
3. I was not certain whether the text should be placed at the top of the page / (↗) or in the middle. (↘)
4. Young people often experience pressure from outside influences to conform to certain trends, / (↗) particularly when they get into high school. (↘)
5. He could have told his mother that he had spent the evening studying, / (↗) but it would not have been the truth. (↘)
6. The man was not sure whether to pick the striped tie, / (↗) the green tie, / (↗) or the purple tie. (↘)

Chapter 9 Pausing

▸ Step 1

1. Although the Greeks were credited with the first Western democracy / neither women nor slaves had the right to vote.
2. During the debate / the woman proved that Jason's argument was flawed / thereby embarrassing him in front of everyone.
3. Those pineapples were / in my opinion / the best fruit that I had ever tasted.
4. Many critics believe that modern movies lack what early movies possessed / namely / a strong plot and good actors.
5. Common pets in American households include birds / cats / and dogs.
6. Nevertheless / I still do not agree that animal testing is worthwhile.

▸ Step 2

1. His ability to track creatures across long distances / enabled the man to compete in an annual competition / where contestants tracked certain animals.
2. Many scientists contend that the universe started with a big bang, / releasing enormous amounts of energy to create the solar systems and planets.

3. In the last three years, / Joe's friends not only supported him during his illness, / but they did everything in their power to make life easier for him / so that he could recover more quickly.
4. Neela, / a foreign exchange student from India, / came from a small village in the mountains that depended almost entirely on farming.

Practice Test 1

Question 1

Sample Response:

One of my goals is to receive my doctorate degree later in my life. I want to receive my doctorate for two key reasons. First, it would make my parents proud. They always stressed the importance of education as I was growing up. Neither of them had the opportunity to get a college education, however. I know that they would be pleased if I could manage such an achievement. In addition, I am deeply passionate about my field of study in philosophy. Getting a doctorate in philosophy would allow me to explore this subject even further.

Question 2

Sample Response 1:

I believe that young people should volunteer for civic work. First, civic work is a social responsibility. Everyone benefits from the community, so it is everybody's obligation to voluntarily help their communities. Secondly, I think young people are more likely to appreciate their communities if they do not receive a monetary reward for it. I have known people who are paid for jobs involving civic work, and they do not have nearly the same enthusiasm as a volunteer has. This is because volunteering teaches young people compassion for others instead of for what they hope to get out of the experience.

Sample Response 2:

I believe that young people should be paid for civic work. Although I think volunteering is good, it is not fair to expect young people to work for their communities without compensation. Many adults who work in hospitals, animal shelters and other areas of civic work get paid for their efforts. Young people should be given the same consideration. Additionally, young people often do not have time to volunteer in their communities. Personally, I am far too busy with homework and other activities to volunteer freely. In order to justify our time spent working in civic affairs, I believe payment is necessary.

Question 3

Sample Response:

The announcement explains that the campus health-food restaurant, Green Acres, will be closing down at the end of the semester. The female student is upset by this decision. She claims that the reason why the restaurant was not popular with the students is because it was not advertised well. She explains that she had seen a total of two advertisements for Green Acres since it had opened three months ago. She also disagrees with the idea that the food was too expensive. She states that she is willing to pay extra for food that is healthy, and she feels most students feel the same way. She concludes by commenting that this restaurant is the only healthy one on campus.

Question 4

Sample Response:

The passage deals with the subject of vaccination. The professor supports the information in the passage by using the example of smallpox to show how vaccinations have been used successfully. She explains that smallpox was a deadly disease 200 years ago until smallpox vaccines were introduced. The vaccines allowed the body to develop a resistance against smallpox through two stages outlined in the reading. First, the body developed antibodies to destroy the disease. This occurred after a weakened form of a disease like smallpox was given to the patient. Then the patient's body stored some of these antibodies in case of future smallpox infections. Through these stages, the body became immune to smallpox. As a result, the professor explains, the smallpox disease has died out.

Question 5

Sample Response 1:

The woman's problem is that her current roommate is keeping her awake at night by talking on the phone. Initially, the man suggests that the woman report her roommate to the R.A. Then he suggests that she switch rooms. I think suggestion two is the better option. First, by doing this, the woman can avoid getting her roommate into trouble. This will keep her roommate from getting angry with her. Also, even if the roommate does stop talking on the phone, it probably will not be for very long. The woman said that her roommate had stopped for a while before, but then started up again. By moving to another room, the woman could keep her roommate happy and ensure that she gets more sleep at night.

Sample Response 2:

The woman's problem is that her current roommate is keeping her awake at night by talking on the phone. Initially, the man suggests that the woman report her roommate to the R.A. Then he suggests that she switch rooms. I think suggestion one is the better option. First, I think it is too much trouble for the woman to move to another room. She should not have to move because of a bad roommate. Secondly, I do not think the roommate will ever stop talking on the phone late at night until she gets in trouble. She needs to learn a hard lesson for her rudeness. By reporting her roommate, the woman would avoid having to move and would stop her roommate's bad behavior for good.

Question 6

Sample Response:

The professor explains how different languages can develop from the same language. Originally, he says that there was one common language spoken by all people. However, when people began to split into different tribes, the languages that each tribe spoke changed somewhat. They became different versions of the same language called dialects. To explain dialects, the professor cites the different versions of English used in the United Kingdom and America. The professor uses as an example Spanish and French. However, he also says that though these languages are different, they still have similarities. This shows that they had a common origin.

Practice Test 2

Question 1

Sample Response:

One person from history that I admire is Harriet Tubman. She was an American who was a slave during the 19th century. I think very highly of Harriet Tubman because she freed so many of her fellow slaves at great danger to herself. Even though Tubman had escaped from slavery, she risked her life to return and help hundreds of her fellow slaves to escape. In addition, she worked hard to give women in America the right to vote. I feel Harriet Tubman is a perfect role model because she risked a lot for what she believed in.

Question 2

Sample Response 1:

I believe that teachers should not be limited in the amount of homework that they can assign. First, such a policy would violate the right of the teachers. Given their close association with the class, only teachers can decide how much or how little homework is necessary to ensure that the class understands the material. Moreover, such a policy might encourage school officials to take further measures to limit the role of the teacher in the classroom. Teachers need to have clear and definite roles if they want to make a difference to their students.

Sample Response 2:

I believe that restricting the amount of homework a teacher can assign would be beneficial. First of all, teachers often assign students too much homework. Even if a student has only half an hour of homework per class, taking five or six classes can result in nearly three hours of homework per evening. This tends to discourage and exhaust students. Additionally, I believe that other activities, like extracurricular activities or jobs, can teach students important skills that homework cannot. Students need to be encouraged to pursue these activities instead of simply concentrating on piles of homework.

Question 3

Sample Response:

The department's announcement states that it will be canceling an upcoming publications class. It explains that the professor who normally teaches the class will be out on extended leave. It also said that there is not sufficient student interest in the class. The male student in the conversation is upset by this decision. He explains to the female student that he knows of a graduate student who could be a great student teacher for the class. He claims that she knows more about publishing than other professors do. He also disputes the claim that there is not enough student interest in the class. He explains that he knows at least ten other students that were planning on taking the publications class.

Question 4

Sample Response:

The reading states that there are two differences between male and female songbirds that affect their songs. The professor explains that one difference is in the RA, which is a part of a songbird's brain that controls song production. She says that the RA is much bigger in male songbirds. She mentions the male zebra finch, whose RA is at least five times larger than that of a female zebra finch. Also, she explains that the brains of male songbirds can make a specific hormone. This allows them to produce more elaborate songs. The professor then says that baby female songbirds that have been given more of this hormone also produce more elaborate songs, proving that this hormone plays a big part in song production.

Question 5

Sample Response 1:

The female student is concerned about an upcoming group presentation for one of her classes. Her friend suggests that she could let her group do most of the speaking, while she does the writing. He also suggests that she practice her portion of the presentation a lot beforehand. If I was the student, I would choose to practice and just do it. First off, public speaking is a necessary skill to have in most professions. I believe the student would benefit if she learned how to do it well now. Additionally, even if she does mess up her speech, I think her professor will likely grade her higher if she genuinely tries to speak instead of not trying at all.

Sample Response 2:

The female student is concerned about an upcoming group presentation for one of her classes. Her friend suggests that she could let her group do most of the speaking, while she does the writing. He also suggests that she practice her portion of the presentation a lot beforehand. If I was the student, I would choose to let the rest of my group do the speaking. As the student stated, there is no way that she can be sure that practice will keep her from messing up. It did not help her in the past. Also, she runs the risk of hurting her entire group's grade if she messes up her part of the presentation. It would benefit her group more if she did the writing instead.

Question 6

Sample Response:

The professor's lecture discusses how carnivorous plants can only grow best under certain conditions. The first condition is soil that is low in nutrients. The professor says that carnivorous plants often die when they are grown by humans. Scientists believe this is because they usually receive too many nutrients. Since carnivorous plants evolved to get all of their nutrients from the insects they eat, soil that is too rich in nutrients is harmful to them. This is why carnivorous plants can only grow in environments like swamps, where the soil is poor in nutrients. Additionally, carnivorous plants require very moist environments. They often die if they dry out. The professor gives an example of a pitcher plant, which requires moisture in order to capture prey.

Compass
Publishing